SECRETS

Novels published by Midnight Fire Media

Your Own Fate
Night on Earth
Dreams Belong to the Night
ShadowWalk
Alarums of Reality

The Janus Clan series:

The Defenseless
The Slaves
Birds Flying in the Dark
At the End of the Rainbow

Poems:

Amos Keppler: Complete Poems 1989 - 2003

(A few of the) novels to be published:

Afterglow Dust
Season of the Witch
Thunder Road: Ice and Fire
Falling
Black Dragon
Red Shadow
Lewis of Modern York

For a «complete» list of current and current future Amos Keppler and Midnight Fire Media projects see the back of the book and the Midnight Fire/Midnight Fire Media web pages.

SECRETS

DESCRIPTIONS OF WHAT CANNOT BE DESCRIBED

by
Amos Keppler

His poems 2003 - 2013

∞

MIDNIGHT FIRE MEDIA
2013

Midnight Fire Media

http://midnight-fire.net/mfm
For more secrets:
http://midnight-fire.net/tps

E-Mail:
amos13@midnight-fire.net
manofhood@yahoo.com

Cover, text, design, premedia, art and photos Amos Keppler

ISBN 978-82-91693-15-6

Contents

CHRONICLES OF A POEM FORETOLD
Spring of discontent

Spring of discontent *ends*

Diversity

I don't have the answer.
I don't think anyone has.
And that's my answer.
That's humanity's one, true calling…
to search for something we'll never find.
We're not here by anyone's design
But our own
Our very nature is to Grow, to learn
Not the hollow pursuits of science
But of ourselves
Each of us experiencing existence
From our own, unique perspective
Learning about ourselves
Thereby learning about existence
Current cultural teaching
The torture of socializing
Is merely braces
Keeping us from gaining insight
If we allow it
We're steered into
Sticking our head into
A narrow hole in the ground
Fooled into picking and choosing
Tiny pieces of ourselves
Tiny pieces Of Reality
Instead of embracing it all
Life is Diversity
Not one single wave

Not even an ocean
But an ocean of oceans.
Deny one part of nature
And your nature
And you deny it all!
Are you a human, roaming Wild
Or are you a sheep
Stewarded (by a shepherd) through cages?
Good and bad, right or wrong
What does it matter
Except as a moral outrage
Of a contained
Mockery of Life
Illusions in a box
Of inhumanity
Experience is the key
Diversity is the lock
Not a lock at all
To Eternity
And it's all just words
Names for something words
Can never describe
We're searching endlessly for
Something we'll never find
And it's good.

Poem for a stormy night

There's a Storm raging outside my windows.
Not just my window
But my windows
Inspiration runs high
Along a crocked line
I adore these stormy nights
With thoughts and possibilities
Passion and Thunder
So far away from the gray day

A dark lodge somewhere
In a nowhere place
Not difficult to reach
Warrior witches dancing nude
Around the hottest fire
There is torrential rain
The fire burns on
There are firemen doing their worst
To put out the fire
With gasoline
They fail miserably
In their rage they drop
An atom bomb on the ring
The star of fire
More gasoline feeding the fire

The day after is never the same
After this, who can say
There isn't life out there?
The sun rises in the east
Setting in the west
Night begins anew...

And the blood gives up its secrets

RAGS

A man stands on a stage
Dressed in rags
He keeps screaming at the
Adulating audience
This is how the world is
The world is not people in suits
Bubbling Champagne
In a luxury resort
The world today
Is people in rags
People going HUNGRY
Feeling the Hunger
In every piece in their guts
Sick to their stomach

A woman kneels in the street
Puking her guts out
This is the world
This is the illusion we cling to
We drown in vomit
We dress in rags
In the ivory tower
Of our mirage

Rows of puppets walk through
The desert of our hopes
They are not humans
They are not alive
They are pretenders
To the life of giants
The sun burns the skin
Covered by holes
The rags protect us
From what we don't need
Protection from
A dress is a rag by another name

FULL MOON

I walk outside in the night
Under the full moon
I've never seen the moon so… full
I walk into darkness
I walk into the shadow
I walk into the light
The silver light
I feel my sinews stretch
I feel my fangs grow

The shingle is glowing in silver
I've never seen the shingle so… bright
In the emancipation of me
I see the bright shadows of myself
Luminescent leaves are glowing in green
I've never seen leaves so… green
The night is not silver
It's not shadow
It's not bright
It's all of the above
I feel air fill my lungs

THE DREAMING

I dream of the forest in the rain
I dream of the endless, twilight summer
At the end of time
The world is Shadow
Bathed in orange light
Tongues of the devil fill the air
Of the moving spirits

They speak
And what they speak is *fire*
I dream of the path without end
And it is no dream
I dream of creatures with fangs and claws
I see them roam the Earth
It's the dream of open eyes
Of a place where trees have no wounds
No juice drowning the Earth

They sing
The fangs and claws of the Earth
The running two-legged creatures
Without name
The hunters without guilt
Haunted by the few bright spots of the world
By the false light of day

They howl at the moon
They burn in the fire
In their own molten sea
Yes, this is no dream
This is the Dreaming
The Dreaming is real
The dreaming is true
I know how it is
I know that it is
I know the Moon and the Sun
Dance their howls in the sky

NOTHING HAS CHANGED

Nothing has changed but for the worse
Lifting cranes are signs of human life
A man says to the adulated masses
Changes for the better, the man says
Activity of destruction is proof of strength
What maniac is this man
Who are the maniacs believing him
Walk down the streets every day of your life
And you see them smile, see them hiss
And it is all the same
Nothing has changed but for the worse
What is changed is nothing more
Than more of the same

This is the life
The pretence of life
We are sold every day
The times they are not changing
People are not on the move
The masses stand still
And bask in the light of
The kind words and a gun
As long as everybody's happy
Why bother?
Nobody gives a shit, man
The adulated masses keep applauding
The kind words and the gun
It's all the same

Our sons and daughters are
Ours to command
And they join us
In the queue of mediocrity and slavery
It's the way of the world
The world never changing
There is a light shining somewhere
Illuminating nothing
Black and White?
It's all the same
Well-fed slaves
Fear the freedom
They don't want
And everything is great
Eyes never open
Eyes open never stay open
Never turn to fangs, turn to claws
Water never becomes blood
The blood never gives up its secrets
And nothing ever changes
The woman on the dais hisses
But what is seen is the smile
Nothing but the smile
And the smile is what is returned
The smile and the hiss
It's all the same

SECRETS

Secrets
Buried under bridges
In the dark, murky currents
Of its shadow
Blood
Boiling in fire
Secrets are the true world
In the illusion
There is no blood
No fire
And it is as real
As a greedy man's heart

Secrets are the world
The currents of the world
Flow in the shadows
Fake are the houses
Of plastic, steel and concrete
As real as
A piece of paper
In a river of fire

The mysteries of the world
Are not hidden
Only conveniently overlooked
They are for everyone
Everyone wanting them
A taste of blood
A touch of fire
And they're there

Only the mundane life
Holds no secrets
The mirage we're fooled
To hold on to
We exist as
Clerks, sheep and ants
When we can be Human
We are bloodless corpses
When we can be Fire
We are the secrets
Of the world

MURDER SPREE

Why haven't I gone on a murder spree
On the suspecting world
What is it that is fucked up within me
Where did I go wrong
It is what every human being
Should have done, should be doing
Drowning it in water
Drowning it in fire
Am I this domesticated
This civilized
This repulsive, tamed creature

From cradle to grave we're told
The unimportant is important
That the important is not
That countless atrocities are not atrocities
But meritorious acts
We become the lie, become the atrocity
And all that is human is drowned in garbage
All that is life turns poisonous and stale
So we do our chores, unmake our choices
Even the few not insane
Are touched by it
Irrevocably haunted by its mark
On their skin

The Kingdom of the Dead

I see it all around me
I see it in the streets
I see it in the creatures
Pretending to be human
Walking the streets
I see the cathedrals of Civilization
Wherever I go
I see the death of spirit
The death of fire
The absence of humanity
Even in the distant wilderness
Planes are passing
Above my head
Civilization can never be left behind
As long as it there
I see it wherever I turn my eyes
The Kingdom of the Dead

Had to pee before I pee on myself
Had to eat because I am hungry
Had to walk because I want to walk
Had to live, because I am Human

For millennia seers have prophesized
About a distant kingdom
Where Death is in every corner,
Every nook and cranny of the world
Where Life is Destroyed on every level
Where humans are hardly more than ghosts
Sickly, pale creatures of doom
Stumbling through a gray, desolate landscape
Into the twilight
That kingdom is distant no longer
That kingdom is today
It's not a mythical kingdom
In the fairy tale of religion
It's real and tangible
A hell of our own making
Prophecy fulfilled
Rejoice humanity
The Final Days are finally here

Have to pee before I pee on myself
Have to eat because I am hungry
Have to walk because I want to walk
Have to live, because I am Human

THE SINGING RIVER

The river is singing. And when you see a bear hunting fish in that river both the river and you come even more alive. You feel the beyond powerful fire of the hunter in the midst of water. As always there are no contradictions. Fire, water, air, soil, infinite Space, filled with Life. And here these idiots come and want to lessen that, to reduce it to numbers, to insignificance. I feel sadness, of course, but what I most of all feel is Rage, boundless Fury. How can I not??? How can anyone feel anything but disgust with the modern world, with civilization. Are they all just people with helmets covering their head, their eyes, ears and mouth and nose and skin, or is it something worse?

What is it going to take? How bad must it be before at least a lot of people are waking up? My fear, my rage is, of course that when Mega City is a reality they will feel, see that as perfectly normal. And it will be!!!
Each new generation is taught new techniques of enslaving themselves.
One generation's nightmare is the next one's dream, in the nightmare world of deception created by civilization.

It's getting worse, and yet people calling themselves radicals insist on using old, unproven, disproved methods.

The river is singing.
To me.
And to all.
There are those who listen.
But they are not necessarily acting and raging because of it.
The wild is compartmentalized, pocketed and filed away.
And only very few people calling themselves Human Beings give a fuck.

I can feel the raging river.
I am the bear raging its roaring streams
You are, too

And I'm so pissed because we have to experience that through a filter.
Even when we're There, the filter is with us, inside us.

That's why civilization will always go with us, no matter where we go...
As long as civilization is There.
Civilization is the filter.
civilization is the chains imprisoning us in dead rock.
Civilization is the noise, keeping us from hearing a feather hitting the ground.
Civilization is the lashing of a whip hitting a naked back.
The sound of a key turning in the prison door.
The dam delaying the river on its journey to the sea.
Civilization has no room for life, for Human Beings.
Civilization's servants are drones, robots, androids, cyborgs, machines.
That's the only purpose civilization will ever allow.
No singing river, no dancing bear, no fire glowing in the night.
Civilization is defining present day humanity
Someone says.
And they are right.
Since modern humans are drones, robots, androids, cyborgs, machines.
The river's singing, is haunting me in the night, and won't let go.
That's good.
I'm burned by the night's glow
And I am the dancing bear around the fire river
Flowing through steel, plastic and poison
Even in this, oh, so limited world there are no limits
I am pissing in the singing river every second of the day
I am touching its keys
Playing its music
How can I not?
How can anyone?

THE POET

I sat there
Without a single thought
In my head
It dragged on for minutes
Hours, days, years
And I feared it was gone
I feared I was gone
Down the drain of mediocrity
I despaired and I couldn't even despair
I even stopped listening for the silence
In the air
In the wretched night
But suddenly
Something happened
Nothing happened
I just sat there
And suddenly it was there
Like it always is
Coming from nothing
From the big nothing
We all stem from
And I listened
To the silence in the night

Words born of dreams
Dreams born of life
Life created from nothing
Form from nowhere
I sat there, staring at my face
My demonic face
A face behind a gate
A wide-open gate
Born of twilight
Blue sky, dark sky
Fire born of Earth
Reaching for the eternal night
We are the stuff
That dreams are made of
We are the fire
In the eternal night

There is a train
Leaving the station
There are no rails
Ahead of it
But it's leaving still
The gates are wide-open
As wings flap like dreams
A train isn't moving
No one in a train is moving
This isn't a train
This is body and mind, time and space
Strands of night and fire
Creating itself from nothing

EARTH

This is the world
The world is Magick
The world is nature
Red and green, blood and rain
They claim the world is walls
Bricks, mortar and polished wood
Constructs piercing the sky
But it's not
The walls don't belong
They are the disease
Poisoning the world

The world is Magick
Touch a brick wall
And it isn't there
Touch the air
And it's there
Touching your mind
Touching your core
You can't wave a magick wand
And make everything better
You can't kiss a wound
And make it heal
But you can touch
The Magick within
The flow and ebb of the world
And thus move the world
As the world moves you

The world is nature
Wild, raw and unruly
Try to control it
Try to steal its gold
And like mercury
It slips through your fingers
It's a waterfall
Beyond all pipes
A Storm leaving all constructs
In ruins
Everything built to last
In constant disrepair

The Thunder Road is not a place
But a state of mind
The human beings
Walk this road
Not a road
With its turns and twists
The Long Walk
Without beginning
Without end
The ebb and flow of time
Are moving through us
Life in all shapes and forms
Is boiling in our veins
The world is a rainbow
We are the rainbow of the world

WORDS WE WON'T EXPLAIN

Civilization destroys everything
Making Life worth Living
We are the stuff dreams are made of
We are the edges cutting deep
We walk everywhere, as if we own it
Because we know
We can own nothing
We laugh at the heart of adversity
And there is a lot of it
To go around

We are humans
They want machines
We want no more bricks in the wall
No more wheels
No more machines
The land is not ours
It belongs to no one
Or nothing, except itself
There is the ancient dance
And that is all there is
That is the boundless
Infinite, eternal
Life that is the Universe

There is the creature
The shadow in the wilderness
Breathing life into fire
I walk through burning cities
As wings flap like dreams
Dreams die and are destroyed
In the rotten heart
Of the stone city
Dreams are born
In the midst of hopelessness
In the ever present cauldron
Of the human being
Inside flesh, inside mind
Burning flesh, burning mind

Civilization
The theater of
Absolute cruelty and tragedy
Marches on
A nail is piercing
Another heart
Just another day
On the stage
At the theater of cruelty
The river runs by
As twilight set
In the places
Of the walking dead

Ice cuts into your heart
And you take that ice
And make it glow
And there is a lot of it
To go around

WHAT ENDURES

The Earth is gone
The Sun is gone
The Galaxy is gone
Even that universe is gone
The Universe endures
Humanity endures
The Shadow endures
With no beginning or end
There have been many universes
There will be many more
On an unending strand
Of Night and Fire
Ancient scenarios are replayed
Time and time again
With a twist or none

The Universe is vast
Beyond measure
Beyond imagination
Various planes of existence
Interact and mingle
Creating more new
And different realities
There are many worlds
There is only one
This one
This vast one
Life rose with the Universe
It's rising still
Learning, growing
With the tree, the tree of Life

Matter is boiling
Energy is cooling
Into something unrecognizable
There is no matter
There is no energy
Life is Shadow
And the shadows travel the Universe
Travel the unending path
The invisible labyrinth
Labels have become meaningless
Like they've always been
There was Fire
There was Shadow
There is still

The molten sea is rising from itself
Beneath the horizon
Beneath itself
There is flesh
There is spirit
There is Shadow
There is the dance
The ongoing, unending dance
Making a turn
On a road already turning
Fire moves through itself
With itself, is itself
Fire endures

AT NIGHT

I love the quiet darkness
It responds to something
Deep within me
Something deep within me
Responds to it
Its many candles
Its oozing torches

At Night
I walk through burning cities
As wings flap like dreams
I walk through forests
Free of domestication
I breathe the pure air
Of mountains free of garbage
At Night I live

I'm pulled in a thousand directions
Simultaneously
And they're all one
They're all myriad
I'm the shadows in the night
I'm a witch
I'm a human being
I'm Night
At night
I *am*

LIGHT OF DAY

In the light of day
I die little by little
In this light of day
The gray, inhuman light
Called civilization
A collective tailspin, suicide run
Of horrible proportions
The hostility strikes you hard
From your first breath
A sickening, palatable queasiness
Attacking you on all levels

The world is a garbage can
At the start of the twenty-first century
(western, christian time-frame)
On Earth there is a white light,
Illuminating everything,
A garden where no weed is growing,
Tended by its gardeners.
Everything is neat
Everything forgotten
Even the forgetting itself
The deep night nothing but
A forgotten memory

DEEPER NIGHT

We arrived at dusk
On the high ground
In the forest
We made preparations
We drew circles, drew stars
On the forest ground
Drew inside and outside
Our own being
What is made without
Is made within

Witches and outcasts
The witches that are outcasts
Gather from near and far
It's a quiver in the ground
In the depth of night

A song is rising from hungry mouths
Seeking sustenance, seeking blood
Boiling in the veins
Fire is rising from the dry ground
From the wet, moist places
Where our Self hides
Hiding no more
Sounds of the night reach us
From the farthest, closest
Corner of the Earth
Thoughts come bidden
From the heart of fire
Where are we
If not here
What are we
If not Human
We are strands of night and fire
The deepest recesses of human life
This is who we are

Here is hard soil
Soft as swaying grass
Here is soft soil
Hard as shaking mountains

We have been pulled here
To this tall mountain
Pulled into the witch's circle
The dance around the ghostly fire

And there
As the fire rose
As the Shadow rose
We touched something
Something ancient
Something beyond today
Something profoundly human
A quality sorely lacking
In today's wretched existence
Magick is returning from its long exile
A violent Storm
So long in waiting
The world is no longer dead
But burning with the strongest fire
Tempered in the blackest night
The hottest blood

The moment we returned to the city
To civilization
We were attacked
By a swarm of killer metal wasps
Festering on our skin and mind
Destroying us from the inside out
I'm sick to my stomach
Of civilization
That's good

We keep hearing
The sound of night
We're still here
In the forest
In the fire
In the Shadow
Living the life
Of the Human Being

COMPLETE

There is the sound of a piano somewhere
Brittle, musical discords
Playing my heart
I saw a dead man stand in the driveway
He stared at me
With his sockets without eyes

I passed a dead man walking
On a cloudy day
He touched me slightly
With his icy fingers
I felt pain
As fire burned my veins
The park garden with its dead trees
Imprinted itself in my mind
My eyes hurt
Ember lit my eyes

I was complete
I walked into the world
And saw Death for the first time
And was thereby incomplete
And then I was complete
And then I was flying
Incomplete
Complete

THE END OF THE BEGINNING

The man is dead
A walking dead
A ghost breathing
The wind is bringing
Fake rot and all bad things
The child is dying
Breath by breath
The man is dead

We found a fish on land
Gasping for breath
A human being kicking it
With a large stick
Inside I felt the warmth
From the kitchen
Turning me inside out

Steam rises from the campfire
On the rise behind our tail
Our tail wagging
Like branches in the night
Invisible, like ghosts breathing
There is no kitchen
There are no walls
Only the child screaming
The child is dead
The man is not

TRUE DEATH

Do you want to die
Do you enjoy dying

There is a loud crack in the horizon
Nobody hears
Ghosts of marble and stone
Pass the time
Repeat their chores
Dull their heart
Pain is a crack in the horizon
And it is a wonder to behold

Stories are told
About the greatness of mankind
What we have accomplished
What we once were
There is a melody, a tune in the shadows
No one in the pitch-black day
Can ever see
I walk, and my feet hurt
I lift and my hands are sore
I think, and my mind reels
From the nothing of it all

Do you want to die
Do you enjoy dying
I ask the passing ghosts in the streets
I ask the executive director
In the pitch-black darkness of the day
I see
Stumbling bodies with all their flesh gone

I see ruins of the walking dead
And my heart swells with joy

TIGHTROPE

Night surrounds me
I'm walking a tightrope
Of Life and Death
Shadow and Mist
Left is down
Right is down
And I know
The rope can give
Any second, now

The stream becomes a torrent
A flow I bring with me
On the endless run
Thunder in the distance
The song of the wild
Inside me
The wild beast snarling
At the still waters

There are doors passing
There are no doors
Doors to walk through
Through open air
I cut the rope beneath my feet
And I don't fall
But fly through the night
Like a bat or a wolf
Fangs and claws of the Earth
The howl of the wolf
Echoes in the night

The tightrope quivers
Beneath my feet
In the darkest night
Life and Death
Shadow and Mist
It's all one
It's all Myriad
I live, I die
A millions times
I swim the torrent
Of the thousand seas

SOAKED IN BLOOD

He picked the chips from her pocket
They were soaked in blood.
He saw her as she crossed the street
And he followed her into the dark, narrow alley
He grabbed her from behind
And stabbed her repeatedly in her back
The soft sound of the blade
Slipping in and out of her flesh
Echoed in his ear
Unable to utter a single scream
She turned limp in his hands
He let go of her leaking body
As it fell to the ground
He bent down over the hot body
He picked the chips from her deep pocket
They were soaked in blood

He pulled her skirt down her wet thighs
Exposing her rusty cunt
He pulled his skirt down his slippery thighs
Exposing his thick and hard cock
He fell on his knees, lifting her swinging hips
And fucked the broad in the dark alley
Eating the soaked chips
Picked from her deep pocket
She was tight and juicy
She tasted like autumn strawberries
In a field of yellow leaves
It is a rare thing
To find a meal so full

Such is the man said the man
Walking his bright path
Illumination is the key to the man
I search and I find a tree
With the most delicious fruit
I find cut off heads on poles
Such is the woman said the woman
Walking her illuminated path
Bright light is the key
I search the kitchen
I find the most delicious meat
Filled with blood and guts
I live in sin, says the human being
I walk the paths no one else dares walk
There is a castle somewhere
Surrounded by poles impaling human heads
I walk inside, penetrating the belly of the beast.

I bear the child in my belly, says the woman
I carry it forth, and I place it on the stone
The stone of blood
The knife cuts through tender skin
On the stone of blood
I sacrifice the child
I sacrifice the world
Thus is reason, thus is calm
I beget what I have
The nothing of the cave
In which I live

The man and the woman
Find the ripest tree
They gut it like they would a pig
Bathing in blood
Reveling in the air they breathe
The moisture they swim
They taste the strawberries on their lips
Their wet, wet lips
Berries ripe and full
Taste of rust and dawn

A LIFETIME

It's raining
It's a full moon
Peeking at me
From the edge
Of the horizon
A sky cut in half
A sky cut in full
I took a bus trip today
A bus trip is a lifetime

I stumble through the city
Its poison and horrible noise
It's raining
The neon lights blind me
But doesn't dazzle me
A bus trip is a lifetime
For someone
Not truly present at the bus
Living lives of
Creativity and imagination

I'm running through the forest
My steps so light, so confident
I'm at peace
Not the peace of the grave
The existence of civilization
Where nothing ever changes
But the ever-expanding harmony of creation
I made a journey this moment
This eternal moment

STAGNANT WATERS
(This year's christmas poem)

You're drugged, man
Drugged by chemicals
Drugged by assurances
Others give you
Of a good life
And never more than these days
During fucking christmas

You're all just a bunch
Of fucking slaves
Owing allegiance to masters
To people with
No allegiance to you
At all

Take a pill to wake up
Another to fall
Even more
Asleep
Dull your mind
Dull your senses
Languish your body
Sit down in front of the television set
Open a newspaper
And read it with
Your head under your arm
Fool yourself into believing
It's all okay

christmas
Floating on a pink sky christmas
Any christmas
Constitution days of various schemes
Sports arrangements
Popcorn and blood
The old gladiator scheme
Watch others live
Don't live yourself
Live through others
Dream others' dreams

Falling asleep with open eyes
That should be hard...
Shouldn't it?
Even in this vast, tiny pool
Of stagnant waters

Christmas is shit
Christmas is bullshit
Nationalism is horrible
Civilization is crap
Is a trap
Taking from you
Your ability to think, dream and live
The most valuable thing a human being
Can ever possess
Returning only trinkets
And pink clouds
So, what *are* you doing, man
Your time being sand
Stumbling to your local
Garbage disposal unit
With your eyes closed

FADE AWAY

Fade away
Into the living death
Of modern slavery
A child is put on a train
And never leaves it
It runs around a little
Jumping a few times
As an adolescent
Until fading away

There, in the deep shadow
Of the forest we pass by
The train passes by
Are glimpses of the life
The fire we are born
To become
We reach out to touch the forest
From the closed windows
Of the train
Even in the bleak, unnatural
Existence of the city
The primordial forest
Is there with us

We feel it
We touch it
No matter where we go
We touch the passion
Buried deep within
Any human being
All our lives
We are forced
To be something
We are not
If we let it happen
In a world of mediocrity
Terror, oppression and organized tyranny
We strive to hold on
To the core buried deep
Within ourselves
Most persevere a few, brief years
Until they fade away

A painter needs to paint
A writer needs to remain
The Storyteller of the ages
Keep telling stories
As deep as the ocean
And ever keep seeking other things
The foreign beach
Not only beyond the horizon
But the burning sun
Of our seething dreams

But we fade away
Fade away
Into the cesspool
Of mundane existence
The modern slavery
We are trained to uphold
Where we are trained to die
To fade away
Long before our heart
Stops beating
This is the celebrated
Existence of today
A mockery of the life
We are born to live

Yes, this is the truth
Live with it
Don't die with it
Life will always be found
Outside the churchyard
Nothing is more important
Than to experience the world
To escape the spires of the dead
The tombstones where humans rest
There is no other worthy cause except this
Nothing truly matters
As long as we exist under the thumb
Of the spiritual death personified

So a painter paints life
Paints death, paints fire

Paints nothing
And the more nothing
He or she paint
The more accolades it brings
From the applauding dead

There is truth in words
A storyteller tells

Today storytellers are demeaned
Every second of their bleak existence
The more lies they tell
The more celebrated they are
This is the world of today
This pale, hollow existence
This spare part enduring hell

Yes, find comfort, find despair
In the fact that the truth
Is out there
That there is life out there
Find the quiet, menacing desperation
Deep within the forest of your being

Stare into the dark deep night
Of daylight gray
Long enough
And you see the Fire

A Human Being
Will do *anything*
To not fade away

THREE STEPS FROM ZERO

Three steps from zero
There was a man getting blasted by a giant beetle.
I got to walk the walk
From here to nowhere
Tut tut squeaked the ant man
Jumping up and down
Like a giant beetle

In the land of zog
There was singing
And hardly anything else
An even tone
Whispering nothing
A boat sailing a sea without waves
Nice weather today said the woman
Wearing the giant Kleenex apron

A girl is singing in the rain
Under a deep blue heaven
Tjoggie thugg she grins
In her coffin
The undertaker takes
One long hard look
At the queue outside
And quits her job screaming
Her falsetto howl

She hands out cyanide
To everybody outside
And tells them to take care of it themselves
And she takes off for the road
Walking like a frog
On the giant, writhing snake
Jumping in joy for a drop of rain

FOREST STORM

I rest on my back
On the dry forest bed
During yet another storm
I look up
As the wind
Catches the treetops
Making them paint
Patterns in the sky

I walk among the trees
I hear them cringe and squeak
I hear them cry out
In the Storm

I rest on my belly
On the wet forest bed
During the stormy rain
I look down
As the water
Catches the soft soil
Painting beautiful images
On the ground

I crawl among the trees
Bathing in their blood
I feel them growing
In the rain

There is a ghost
Of an echo
In the depth of the forest
In the stinking moors
In the moist space
Between the trees

I run through the forest
In pitch darkness
Stepping in-between
The dry twigs
On the ground
The dry twigs
Crying a warning
To my rapidly moving feet

In a recess
Somewhere in shadow
There is no sound
But the whispering trees
I go there
And I hear the silence
Of the raging Storm
I rush towards the open spot
In the forest
Never forgetting
The quiet darkness
In the shadows

CHRONICLES OF A POEM FORETOLD

(Carpe Noctem 2005-02-27 and onward)
The spring of discontent.

THE POPE IS DEAD

The pope is dead
A bloated corpse
Among the living
Burn the bible
We burned the bible
In the deep night
Showing our contempt for
The walking dead
The pope is dead

This is a man admired
And worshipped by millions
What does it say about them
What does it say about
Their humanity
Their sense of worth
Are they human at all
Or just a swarm of unthinking puppets

The bible burns
Leaving the sound
Of angry wasps
Tear the image of the pope
It's no big deal, really
It's just an ignorant
And intolerant old man
The pope is dead
And all Human Beings
Celebrate his passing

OPEN WOUNDS

We are bleeding
From a thousand small wounds
Wounds staying open
From a very early age
And as we grow up
They become a river

Wounds inflicted never closes
It takes days to heal a wound
And before that happens
Another has come
To take the old one's place

An invisible knife
A blade formed of empty air
Cuts malleable flesh
Hardening it until it is soft no more
A razorblade sword guts the soft belly
Laying it all open for the kill
Bleeding dry the thousand open wounds

A man walks down the street
He loses one drop of blood
For every step he takes
Many drops make an ocean
And the river becomes a waterfall
Leaving only dry husks
In the river of souls

The desert of mankind
Reaches for the horizon
Leaving only small pools of life
Every oasis so small
That only a minute of heat
Makes it go away

Life is okay, you tell yourself
It's not great
It's not bad
You wander around
In a stupor
Through the desert of mankind
Wondering if this is all there is
All there is

So where do we go
In this place of countless dull knives
I stick a needle in my arm
Attempting to find some blood
But there's nothing there
I repeat the operation many times
Until my body is a crater
Of bloated pinpricks
I howl my misery
As my voice turns to a whisper
And howls no more

LIKE A GOOD GIRL

In the darkness of the day
There are chores
We are told to do
We are made to do
And I do them
I do them every day
Like a good girl

Keep the wheel turning, they tell me
And I oblige them
Reluctantly in spirit
Eagerly in fact
The wheel of pain is turning
And we're all dancing its tune
Just like a good girl

Do your chores and be happy
They tell us candidly
Telling the worst kind of lies
And we all do them
We believe them
Because we want to
Like a faithful dog
Like star-eyed boys
Calling ourselves men

We know it's not true
We know there is no holy grail
At the end of the rainbow
But we keep chasing it
Keep enjoying the stick and carrot game
Never truly speaking back
Like a polite, obedient boy
Like a good girl
The very picture of well-behaved youth

In some recess we're all drinking tea
Hiding from the harsh, cruel, fake world
Nauseas, sick of it all
Tasting the winds of change
We go to bed every night
Still there
Still the well-behaved boy
The good girl

MYSTERY SONG
(Call the Shadow)

There is a discord in the air somewhere
As we stumble through the desert of mankind
A resonance true, in a world of lies
A Mystery Song drawing in everybody
Listening to it, seeking its distant shores
The tongues of fire you feel inside
Are striking the shores of the foreign beach
And as you reach out a hand
Reaching for your heart
It's right there inside you

I call the Shadow, the eternity of me
From the vastness of the Universe
Both there and here, inside and outside
And the third eye chasing through the darkness

The wind whispers in my ear
The spirits speak to me
So many, so many grains of sand
An infinite, broken and unbroken string of Shadow
We swam through the long and wet darkness
To the seething, unending fire below
We still do

We float in the Chaos of our own
Fevered, half-realized thoughts
There is no stability
Equilibrium is an illusion
An egg balancing on its point
There is Chaos, and Night and Fire
Write a word on a wall
Give it meaning, give it Chaos
Burn the bloated corpse
A body is hidden in the darkness

A body hides in the Night
Peeking at the campfire from the darkness

This place is Fire
This very place is consecrated
To ancient Night, to pagan Life
Forever dedicated to Shadow
Broken pieces of tomorrow
The fire is the only sound
We can hear

LAUGHING WALLS

The walls laugh
They are laughing at us
The joke is on us
We raised the walls
Around ourselves
Inside ourselves
We closed ourselves off
From the world
From ourselves
The walls laugh
They are laughing at us
The joke is on us
Freedom was lost
At the first wall.

I'm entering a room filled with old piss
It feels pleasant, somehow, it feels real
In a world of pretence and forgery it rings true
The cleaning man enters the room
Accusing me of desecrating his altar
I reply by telling him that
You can't desecrate anything
That's already dirty
I leave the room stinking of old piss
The harsh smell leaving with me
Leaving the cleaning man
To his laughing walls

The laughing walls are with us
Wherever we go
It haunts us even in our greatest moments
Making it all ring false, making it all wrong
I go to the highest mountain, the deepest forest
And it's still there, in my ears
Filling my ears with cotton does me no good
It's still there, louder than *ever*

I run, panic choking the breath from my lungs
I fly away, and my wings turn brittle and black
I scream my despair from the top of my lungs
And there is only an echo of a response
I sweat, I bleed, I run
I stumble and fall, exhausted and defeated
A shell of a man
Joining all the others
Between the laughing walls

POISON

Poison might be sneaky
Might be unattended for a long time
As it works on you
As it breaks down your body
As it's diluting your mind
Killing your mind
While your body is still somewhat walking

There is a stable with shiny exterior
All the horses inside are groomed and well fed
It might be hard, truly hard to even glimpse
The locks on the door

The horses are taken out regularly
Exercised every morning and day
And they're groomed and fed
In the evening they rest
At night they sleep
There are sores, there are wounds
There's nothing to it
Everything is promptly taken care of
The next day the horses are once more
Fit for fight, fit for riding, fit for grooming
Poison is healing poison
And everything is well

Poison breaks you down
Killing you softly
Not one painful gasp
But a prolonged scenery
Of torture and death
The horses are groomed and fed
And they are content
The stable is their coffin
And they know no other life

THIS FAIRYTALE NIGHTMARE

Cinderella sits in her castle, in her ivory tower
Hardly ever recalling her time of strife
Eating well all day, still starving
Dancing with her prince
Eating her heart out
Dancing with her prince

I'm still me, she insists before the mirror
Every day she says these words
As if she truly believes them
Her lips move
But there's no sound
No sign of words actually being spoken

She's wandering the old, dusty halls
Day out and day in, day and night
Unable to sleep
The food and wine are bland
She wonders where are the delights
She was promised

She eats, walks and sleep
As the nightmare progresses
As she slowly, inevitably
Is turning into one more of the castle's
Many refined unmoving marbles
Resigning herself to a life in hell

GHOST OF LIFE

The marble sky above is falling
It hits my head, making my head bleed
I traverse the desert of mankind
Bleeding from a thousand wounds
A million of my fellow bleeders
Walk with me there, on the hard-packed soil

The desert of mankind surrounds me
No matter where I go, where I run
Tall tombstones shadow the Sun
Closing off access to the living Earth
Ghosts of human beings strain my eyes
Making it hard for me to breathe
I need to strain my eyes real hard
To glimpse a ghost of life
Among all the living dead

Dead eyes glare at me
Glare at my seeking eyes
What's wrong with me, they ask
Why do I stare at them
With my non-envious eyes
They see pity in my glance
And anger flare in their frozen hearts

I see, I find, I keep seeking
I walk street up and street down
Searching for words of life
And tonight, perhaps tonight only
I find it, find a glimmer of
Something not dead

There is a wind in the streets tonight
Something awfully fresh and interesting
I can feel the fear rise in me
The indoctrination of
A thousand eventless days
Makes me want to puke
I look at the shadows between the neon lights
Spotting the dark alley in my mind
I hesitate before plunging headlong
Into that alley, that sign of life
I pull further into the shadows
Feeling more and more at home there

There is an unpleasant haze in there
A mist I can touch and feel
I can see the distant clouds
I can feel them vibrate in me
Telling me the present day horrors of the world
Won't continue
Convincing me that we all won't remain
A ghost of the human being

I'M CRACKING UP

I laugh like a crazy man
Even though I can't say for sure
If the crazy man does indeed laugh
I sit in my sanctum
And dark laughter rises in shadow

The world is doing an upsy turvy
On my freaking desk
And the dance does a table
In the ceiling
It's finally happening

I walk through the rain
Feeling the elation of walking
I get wet
And I no longer get wet
It's a walk where I feel
The thump of each step

There is a mountain ahead
Where we *can* laugh
And truly mean it
And it's all real
I laugh like a crazy man

A SIMPLE STORY

This is a simple story
Of reason and passion
Bigger than the sum of the parts
About a land without kings
Without gods, priests and bosses
There are death and suffering
But not an abundance of it
Poison, spiritual and physical
Is not produced
On an assembly line

There is simple human dignity
Not the travesty pretending
To be that today
There is Freedom
Unqualified, abundant
There is justified hope
That tomorrow will come
And not bring even more
Misery, terror and organized insanity
Humans remain humans
And not automated robots
All these things are gone
And Life has taken its place
That is a simple story of tomorrow
If tomorrow comes

WE ARE THE WITCHES

Surrounded by mist
Seeing nothing but clarity
We are what once was
What this fire-bright night is again
The deep-core bass rumble
Shakes our house
The house of the Earth
The ground beneath our feet

We are told that teeth are bad
That even though we have teeth
We shouldn't show them.
Well, I'm here to tell you
That teeth are good
That teeth are great.

They baptized us witches
Heathens and pagans
Branding us enemies of mankind
Casting a spell of violation and illusion
Over mankind's eyes
They branded us
And tortured and killed us
Slowly
In their quest, in their zeal
To eradicate us
To eradicate the Human Being
From the face of the Earth
But they failed
In mists of time and shadow
They failed
And failed again

We proudly took the name
With which they branded us
And made it our own
We are everything
That is bad, horrible and scary
In their world
Their world of horrors

Our name is Enemy
Our task is horror
We move in shadows
We are not formed in their image
But in our own
Life burns beneath our creepy hides
We endure and live
Beyond the world of destruction
They keep creating

We are the witches
We are what moves and dreams
In Shadow
And in the nightmares of our enemies
And we return what is us
The tiny and crucial pieces
That are us

THE CLIMBERS

They build a staircase of air
Not one of mist and shadows
But of steel and poison
Everything
Everything revolving
Revolving around the staircase
Piercing the sky

The climbers are very busy with their thing
Making everybody busy with their thing
All the official branches of knowledge
Are consumed... with their small thing
Nothing else matters
We mean nothing to you

A tower is climbing the heavens
All the angles are in the right place
It's perfectly proportioned
Oiled and polished and grand
Dispersing all the nightmares of the world
Burying them deep within humanity
Crying, suffering humanity
The victims of the genocide of thought and joy

This is not your bold mountain man
Seeking the mysteries of nature
No, these are the men of destruction
Seeking nothing but the dizzy neon lights
Of the blinding towers of the world
The perfect tower is piercing the heavens

Go to sleep, my child
In the soft bed
At the top of the fake mountain
Teeter at the edge of the Abyss Forever
Without ever falling down
Falling down

Tonight is your night
Today is your day
For what you've worked for your entire life
This is the hour
All your dreams will be realized
This is the moment of fulfillment

Cold, dry sweat awakes you
In the middle of the night
There's no sleep, really
There's no dream anymore
But that of the pale day
Your all-consuming ivory tower
Has taken it all
The perfect tower is piercing the heavens

THE RIVERBED

The man is at the bottom of the river
There are no currents there
The currents pass him by
The riverbed is covered in silt
Silt of polished rock, made metal
It holds on to the man and won't let go
The man's muscles are flexing now and then
But basically they're not used
Not much is happening down there
On the riverbed
I go swimming, says the man
But he never does
Resting his chops there
On the calm shore
Covered by sand
Resting in mud
I go swimming, says the man
I do I do I do
And finally he falls silent
Speaking no more
There is no sound
No fury
There, on the riverbed
Up there, the river runs by
Leaving man behind

WORDS

I know the words I speak
The letters I write
Before I do them
I know them intimately
They come to me as I write them
Sometimes in the distant past

There's a wall of mist somewhere
Where everything is inscribed
Somewhere inside me
In the vastness of reality
The Book of Fate is turning its own pages
In the whirls of fire and Shadow
That is the depth of our existence

Words are mist
Letters are solid rock
Dancing shadows on the edge of consciousness
Three days of rest
Three nights of dream
The Tree of Life keeps branching out
A constant surprise
In the deep well of life

Everything is written
There's nothing more to write
More is added every single moment
Every shred of time there is
My rage and calm
My hopes and fears, desires and dislikes
My painting of the Universe
All that and more
Are written on the wall of Time

The Invisible Labyrinth
Is written before my eyes
The turns and twists
Dancing on the edge of reason
On the precipice of passion
At the back and front of my head
The future and past are written
Simultaneously

I go flip flop where
The Thunder Road makes a turn
And I discover that everything
Is flop flip
Out there, in the whirlwind
Of reality

I can hear when the Storm blows
Because that's where I live
There is nothing out there
Except what we bring with us
When we reach out to infinity
And go where we're not supposed to go
We find everything
We could never see before
The whirlwind blows
In the four and thousand
Corners of the shadow world

So I know the words I speak
The letters I write
I know them better
Than the back of my hand
I see my hand
I feel my hand
But it's just one
Just one single brush
In the multitude
With which I paint my Story

THE EBONY PATH

I walk through night
I cannot sleep
I am restless
I am endless
I cannot for the life of me
Find the spot in the mist
I cannot sleep

I cannot sleep
So I walk through night
I am the ghost in the night
What you see here
Is here now
A ghost speaking in the night
I am the velvet glove in the night

So I am walking
Endlessly
Through the pitch black darkness
I stare at the ebony path before me
And it turns into shadows and mist
And I can see embers
Dance in front of my eyes

Spring of discontent *ends*.

A LONDON POEM

I walk down
Charing Cross Road
An early day in spring
I notice the scents
Lingering in the air
I feel them invade
My very being
So many
Of the spices of life
Are present here
On these many spots

The girl looked
At her face in the pond
It was the eyes
The eyes that
More than anything
Made her face
«They're really something
Aren't they?»
The older woman said
In the mirror said
«It's like they are
The entire face
Like pools of dark blood
Rising from our depths»

This place of places
Is coming to me slowly
Like a warm, pervasive
Prevalent wave
I notice the old things
I awake from my slumber
I notice everything new
I find what I'm looking for
I find what I keep yearning for
The Shadow grows from me
Reaching out where I
Can feel and touch it
I know again
What I've never forgotten

There are old structures
Not structures at all
In human life
The walls certainly not walls
Keep whispering to us
From corners, edges and shadows
Ghosts cry to us
From the realms
Distant and close
Opening us
To all things

I reach out
And grab the flow of spices
And even though
It keeps flowing
Through my fingers
While I weep
It burns my skin
And touches my Self
As never before
I sit on a bench
On Leicester Square
Enjoying the lovely evening
Fluttering birds' wings
Flap and stir the air
Surrounding us

I walk through the forest at night
The ancient, eternal forest
A girl sits by the fire
I am approaching her
Or I sit by the fire
And she's approaching me
I can never tell
We swim through the Serpentine
All of us
All of us out here
On the Freedom Road

These walls are not walls
But mist and shadow
Not concrete and solid form
But strands of night and fire
There is a house somewhere
A house of horrors
A house of joys
Peeling off modern human armor
Like one would do an orange
Devouring it like
One would an apple
The perceived horrors of freedom
Open wide the secrets
Buried in humanity's past
Opening us to the world
To the world again

So we come here
To these intersections
These crossroads of choice
Seeking what we already have
Finding what we've already found
Realization is a powerful force
In human life
All journeys go everywhere
All travel is inside
So I walk these streets
Hunt these forests
In search for what
Will always be here

A good Journey
Stays with you forever
It echoes like thunder
Through eternity
Dreams are what happen
When imagination
Wants to meet reality

I can taste every grain of salt
Every single flavor
On my tongue
Experience every wave
Assaulting me
The air surrounding me
Is aflame with life

The morning commuters
Look like corpses
As usual
Like skeletons without flesh
Covered in skin
I have been up all night
And still look as fresh
As a flower

I have been here
Only forty-eight hours...
Forever

PULLED-OVER SKIN

I see a dead working horse
Lay still by the wayside
Its eyes are filled with ants
Its body is covered in flies
Its pulled-over skin is broken
In several places
Revealing the yellow bones beneath

There is no meat here
Only dry bones and skin
I wonder if this poor soul
Was ever alive
If soft skin ever caressed
His hurting bones

There is no life here
Not even an echo of one
Nothing but dread, disease and early decay
This is a working horse
Not truly a horse at all
But only a reasonable facsimile
I wonder if there was ever a spirit
In this rotting, empty frame

THE MUSE

I am the Muse
I am the cry
In the wilderness
I feel the heat
In the womb
Of the Earth
I feel the darkness
The Shadow
The bright shadow
In my heart
I rejoice
I celebrate
I live
I Live
In the midst of death

Now
Now, the evening begins
In the heart of life
People meet
On the edge of the night
Celebrating life
In all its forms
We are human beings
We are forgotten fire
We are the essence
Of what was lost
Of what is

A door opens
To our depths
Slams open
Hard
As we drink life
As it fills us
Like air
Where air is

This is mankind
This is what is hidden
Beneath the surface
Of modern existence
We live
In the midst of death

WHISPERS

Whispers
Whispers in the night
Chords
Vibrations
In the wind
Strings of fire
The same as
Strings of night

Life is so much
So overwhelming
At the end of time
I see you
A human being
On the edge of shadow
Strings of life

Eternity beckons
On the edge
Of my vision
I sense it
I feel it
I feel its misery
I feel its joy
Setting me free

I set myself
Free
Free from limitations
Fire fills my mind
Removing
The velvet glove
From my mind

Three years
From the night
Of our souls
I felt life
Rise from the depths
Of Hell
The scent of fire
Burns in my mind

THE CANDLE

A candle burns
On the wooden table
In a room without walls
An unnatural gust
Picks up speed
In the gray city fog
In the merciless daylight wind
A candle flickers and dies

Birds float through the ether
On a wave of warm air
Staying afloat
Even in the still wind
A candle is hardly visible
In this the brightest of days

I lit a candle
A dark flame in the night
I hear chimes in the still wind
Memories of yesterday
Of today
Are close in my core
As a catching in my throat
Makes it hard to breathe

I come here often
I visit here
I live here
It's the place
Of my core
The spot where
I always *am*
This is my home
It's not a place
But a state of mind
I walk here
On the darkest night
The brightest day

There are always embers left
Glowing in the night
In the room without walls

It's time

The entire sea boils
With the water from the sky
The entire sky
I've never before
Seen such a sight
Such a marvelous sight

I hear the silence
Of the inner city
It's palatable
Of falling feathers
I hear the thunder
Of running feet
The noise is gone
I can once more
Hear myself think

The Witch sits down
By his candle
Reading the Book of Shadows
In his head
It's time
Time for Life and Fire and Shadow
And everything in-between
And beyond

I play a flute
Calling from the Wasteland
I read a book
That will always be there
No matter how many
Books they burn
No matter how many
Witches they destroy

I cast a spell
One of Night and Fire
Unbinding the Illusion
Of the World
Opening wide
The eyes of the World
Making it see things
It hasn't seen
For a long time
A very long time
It's been so long
Since we all
Saw the World

It's time, now
For many things
For everything
We never did

The candle is blazing a trail
Throughout the grayish day
Making everything turn
Dark and joyous once more
The souls of the candle
Dance eternally
Around the Dark Flame

INSIGNIFICANT DETAILS

Have you noticed
The smell of fresh bread
In the morning
The warm, pleasant floor
Against your bare soles
I notice the whispers
In the wind
The tiny flashes of fire
In the corner of my eyes
Small things are a precursor
To bigger things
Do you
Can you sense the brush of touch
On the small hairs of your skin
The small and big things
Turning scale insignificant
Are you alive
In the smallest part of your Self

Bury me when I'm dead
Let me lie in the street and rot
Causing a stir
Among the walking dead

A BEAUTIFUL GIFT

I seek them out
As they do me
There are still strangers
Still nomads in this world
Seeking freedom and sovereignty
They gather around campfires
In the lovely night
Preserving life and humanity
In all its countless forms
Keeping the dark flame alive
Against all those
Who would threaten it

Nature, and mist and shadow
That is our home
If we lose contact with that
For too long
We lose ourselves.

We sing in the forest
We call in the wilderness
The call goes out
To everybody
That wants to hear
The fiery song
A beautiful gift
Of uncompromising Freedom
In a world derived of almost anything
Making Life worth Living

HOLE

There's a hole inside of me
A black hole where
Everything disappears
We all have it
Inside
Shouting deafening cries
Burning like molten rock
A sense of something unfulfilled
Of something missing
A horrible pain
A terrible joy
Man has called it many things
They have called it The Abyss
When we stare at it
It stares back at us
As we stare back at it
It widens as we distance ourselves
From the world
It widens as we
Embrace the world
It's there, like we are
With us
Forever
I can feel it burning

What makes us tick, you wonder
What is it really
Is it the grand gestures
The flowering speeches
Or something completely different
I feel it in my gut
Inevitable
I feel it move me
I feel it grow
I feel myself
Yes, this is it
This is who we are

I can hear an owl howl
(and not hoot)
It tingles through the night
It flows up my spine
To the place below

I go deep below
I fall, I fly
I go where the grand gestures
The flowering speeches
Don't go
There are fingers hammering
At the broken piano down there
But there is no sound
My ears bleed
Because of the overwhelming sound
My wings flap in the night
They go where I go
Into the Abyss

WHERE I GO

I go
I go behind the corner
And meet the Shadow
I burn in its face
Its tongue licks my ass
Swallowing my Self whole
And I am It
I found myself
In the places I've never looked

It is peaceful afterwards
If that word has any meaning
A campfire burns
In the two rivers of my ears
Is there a meaning in a word
One in a vision or two
Beyond the corner of the soul

I go where no one goes
And in that space
Where nothing can be
I find myself

Another Life

I dream of blood
I dream of night
I imagine another life
Through drowsy impressions
Images of mist
Dark lighting strikes my eyes
Illuminating my day
Sounds of echoes
I hear the human drum
It thunders beneath my skin
I dream my reincarnation dreams

I chase through the night
Looking for the night
There is silver moonlight
There is fiery fire
A woman plays a violin
A dark vibration
Inside an enchanted forest
I follow the river to its spring
I dream of night
And blood and sacrifice
And murder and eating the heart
Beating inside the warm chest

I reach the river's spring
And the water turns red
And I taste it
Taste the water full and fresh
I dive into the spring
Into the bottomless pit
That is the stormy pond
In the forest
I swim forever
Into the currents
Of its depths
Time loses all meaning
It does
I reach the seabed
At its murky end, middle
And new beginning
I feed on the heart of the Storm
I taste the forbidden fruit
I feast on its nectar
Its indescribable content
And...
And...
I feel it
I feel the splinters in the mind's eye
And the blood gives up its secrets

CLEAR SKIES

Clear skies at night
Night hot and dry
In October
The time of winter
In ancient times
Thirty years ago
Nights with clear skies
Were cold then
So very cold

Feverish Earth is here
The Twilight Storm has come
I see fear in people's faces
As they glance at each other
While passing each other
On dusty streets
I walk outside
And I find myself in a desert
It is summer tonight
And tomorrow
And tomorrow will come

The inmates hammer at the gates
Shaking the bars
It is happening
Feverish Earth fills our hearts
Clear skies open our eyes
Civilization crumbles around us
Rotting on the vine
The future looks bright
So very bright

The air is so clear
Deep as a sky
I stand on a mountain
And can see beyond
The end of the world

The Song of Distant Mars

There is a whisper in airless space
Of a legend, long dead
Of dancing Dust, now still and quiet
I walk among these shiny tombstones
Desperately attempting to recall
The song of distant Mars
Lights blink off and on
In the many windows
In this clean-shaven churchyard
The lights might be on
But there is no one home

This place was cleaned of red dust
Eons ago, countless eons ago
In brutal acts, destroying our spirit
Giant vacuum cleaners keep sucking in
The Red Dust of Mars
In desperate acts to keep it
From reaching our nostrils
Because, you see
The red dust remains
No matter how much
They don't want it to

In space, airless and vast
There is a song we all hear
There is no vacuum, no distance
In either time or space
Keeping us from the blood
Flowing through our veins
The song is sung without mouth
Heard without ears
The song began with a scream
But it doesn't end there
Distant Mars isn't truly
Distant at all

Mars is dead and cold, they say
But I know differently
Claws reach for me through
The dancing dust
Gutting my gut
Cutting me open and ready
I know Mars is teeming with life
Birds flap their wings in the thick air
Fish swim the salty seas
Beasts are climbing its sharp rocks
I know, because I've been there
And one day, soon
I'm going back
Going back again

Fingers Like Rain
(Homage to a Squeamish Art Editor)

Tears
Tears are falling
From a cloudless sky
Dead are the clouds
Dead is the sky

A rotting corpse
Stumbles along a road
Its arm falls off with a thud
The rotting corpse stumbles on
Never once changing
The expression in its eyes

The city is hot
It's a greenhouse
Out there, in here
Heads fall off rotting corpses
On an assembly line
It's baking hot all over
And there's no rain anywhere
Except tears from
A cloudless sky

Garbage cans fill the streets
They are stuffed with rotting corpses
Heads roll on the sidewalk
Eyeballs fall out
And roll on the sidewalk
Great art, great art
A man swinging a machete cries
Grinning his insane grin
How about it, Miss Art Editor
Is this fine art or *what?*

Fingers drop from heaven
They drop like rain
And the rain is like blood
But not blood
It's a thick soup
Of sore skin, puss and poison
And the rotting corpses rot
And the dropping fingers drop
And the rain turns to knives
Cutting off heads wholesale

Restaurant guests
Have a field day these days
Enjoying the finest cuisine
And everything is right
With the world

Closing Door
2005-10-22

The door will close
A pale looking man hisses at you
You walk towards a ferry
A rainy day
When the pale man hisses at you
You look closer at the ferry
The door leading inside
Is closing prematurely
Other people scramble
To get inside in time
But you freeze and stop
The door closes
And the ferry leaves
Leaving you behind

You sit there on the bench
Shaking like a leaf
The ferry eventually returns
The door opens, opens wide
Just like an ordinary door
People leave the ferry
In a somewhat orderly manner
You walk inside in a daze
Not really looking down
At the spots of faded blood
Decorating the floor

You sit down
In the deep, pleasant seat
You glance around you
Studying the other passengers
It's fairly obvious
They cannot see what you see
An ice-cold trickle
Rushes down your spine
You sit there, staring at nothin'
Slowly convincing yourself
There is something
Seriously wrong
With the world

Nine to Five
2005-10-22 - 2005-11-03

Time stretches on
In a bad way
Grinding to a halt
In seconds lasting forever
In a bad way

Long, dreary hours stretch on
One second is an eternity undesired
Mules call for hours not to be
And everything is wrong with the world

In tiny office spaces
In cubicles of existence
Semblance of life
Pretending there are bright spots
In sordid days

Four walls are a sanctuary
Four walls are a prison
Home is a fortress of solitude
Protecting you from the world
Pretending to be the world
Cubicles are ridiculous spaces
Shrinking us
Isolating us
From the world

Dustbins float through streets of ashes
People keep coughing
Attempting to breathe
Attempting to take
That one, crucial step forward

The wind is still
There is not
A single breath of wind
In the world
In a world filled with
The worst garbage there is

Clouds fall below
The mountain peaks
The mules bow their heads
Never looking
Beyond that Gray Fog
Clouding their perception

Cubicles are worms
Crawling beneath the skin
Eating us alive

Water of Fire
2005-11-06

There is death
There is life
And there are rotting corpses
Rotting corpses are stumbling
Through ashen paths
I long for Fire Lake
Its clean and clear water
Where there are
No rotting corpses
Walking around

I ran through the forest today
Through the rain and twilight
Attempting to find
To rediscover Fire Lake
Ending up soaking wet
Wet to the bone
My being flooded with
The water of fire
Flooding life

Yesterday I met a car on the road
I could smell the perfume
On the people inside
From far away
Masking the stink
Yes, even the stink of gasoline
I meet people in the forest
Smelling like roses
Masking the rot in their make up

I long for the water of fire
So frowned upon
In today's world of illusion
And unnatural rot
I bathe in it
It permeates my being
But still the smell of rot
Is stuck in my nostrils

I run through rain and twilight
The twilight comes early these days
It's close
Like the blood in my mouth
I can smell it
As strong as the air I breathe

The Child Killers
Late November 2005

Tony, George and all the rest
Where do you get off
Aren't you pleased
Aren't you content
How many more children will you kill
Before you're done

From the moment they open their eyes
You are there, lessening their lives
You are many, you are never alone
In your zeal to destroy
Any shred of innocence

What goes through your mind
As you sit there
Around the square table
Concocting your insane schemes
Your tyranny of convenience

It gets to us
No matter how spirited
We might be
It gets to us, you know
The shit of the current world
You perpetuate and tend

Aren't you pleased
Aren't you content
How many more candles
Will you put out
Before your day is done

Gets to you
Late November 2005

It gets to you
No matter how spirited you are
It gets to you, you know

You sit there
In your cozy flat
Your current brief-home
Your fortress
Protecting you against
The horrors of the current world
You sit there, in your chair
Shaking in rage

Where do they get off
The self-important assholes
Of the world
Claiming they know everything
Knowing nothing
Except how to destroy and control
Crisis management in a time
Totally out of whack

Bleak thoughts cover you
Like a blanket
Constantly warring against you
Waging war against your true self
Burning on a low flame inside

You know what the world is like
The true world beyond the blanket
You've seen it a thousand times
Experienced it in a million
Wonderful, fleeting moments

But the poison covering the present day world
Gets to you, because it's always there
In full, imposing its overwhelming
Mechanical will on you
It's a dead thing, a machine
And it never rests
It's equal to its lemmings of fans
The marching band of destruction
Blanketing the world

So you do your best
Raging against the machine
Killing it a thousand times
A million nights
The next day it's still there
So you walk these streets of ashes
Of occasional fire
In the never dying hope
That hope will never die

It gets to you
It gets to me
It gets to all of us
Destroying everything
Making life worth living
It's a travesty
Something dead and horrible
The absolute worst nightmare
Of our imagination

You pull yourself up by the hair
Fight yourself back on your feet
Fight yourself back on your feet *yet again*
From the coffin of your spirit
You do it a thousand times
You're dog tired, so tired
That you want to unscrew your head
And let it fall into the grave
The grave of thought, of spirit
And everything truly valuable in this world
The coffin pulls you down
With its ten thousand tentacles
And sleep-inducing words

There is a button somewhere
Somewhere ahead
A key to unlocking the door beyond
A switch that will make it all go away
And you keep pushing on
Keep putting one foot
In front of the other
In the burning desire
That some day one person
Or a group of persons
Will one day find that button
Turn that switch
And destroy everything
Destroying the world
Making sure
Its last day has come

That someone might be you
Never stop searching
Never stop telling yourself
That that person might be you

It gets to you, you know...

Stories
Late November 2005

We dream stories from our first spark
In a world so cluttered and out of it
We still dream the dream of release
Of exquisite fevered visions
In the deep recesses of our mind

There are stories everywhere
In every little glance
In every small gesture
At the corner of a girl's smile
In the deepest recesses of the night

Our imagination is an explosion of thought
A constant supernova in our mind
And the bold among us go where no one else goes
Go to the blood-soaked satins covering our bed
To the screaming forest we run through every darkest hour

We go and meet other creators of the world
The world is a dim recollection in our memory
Until we call upon it and call it home
We pull the world into our grasp
We make it true, we make it real

There is a mist rising from the steamy moor
Ghost and spirits and witches and devils
Dancing on a tripwire of emotion and dark laughter
At the drop of a stone, a flap of a feather
The butterfly wings rise to a storm

In the last half of evening, the beginning of night
We find in our punctured, suffering heart the will to heal
In the third half of night, just after the fire of midnight
We go where no one has gone before us
And dead bodies open their eyes

And tombstones tumble and fall, fall, in a pile of dust
And go bump in the night, and every sound is loud
They grow wings and fly on their broomstick
To that mausoleum at the center, where nothing fails to grow
And nothing and no one is dead anymore

THE WHIRL AND THE WIND
2005-12-15

Wind and wisps of air
Fire twisting in the night
Witches setting into the forest
In search of Life
To the flap of Ravens' wings
Gaps in the air
Sucking in wind
A Storm coming
Giving Life to everybody
Embers paint images
On the whirly night sky
In the very air we breathe
And witches open up to it
Welcome the night
The fire, the wind, the Storm
The stuff dreams are made of
Real as a rock
As the dancing embers
Setting our minds afire

I bring fruit
I always do
Juicy and delicious
Between my teeth
The moon flows behind light clouds
Shining on the bed
Of the deep forest
On our twisting bodies
While we sleep
I see it on the vast sky
And I breathe its hot rays
The Hunter's Moon shines on us all
We dance like embers
Twist like flames
Strands of Night and Fire
Alive in the grayest of days
We are the warrior poets
We give meaning
Where no meaning is
There is a dance somewhere
In the blackest of nights
And we need no food, no water
Except from that most generous of springs
In a whirl of water and wind
We find the vortex of our dreams

The Gift of Winter
2006-01-11

I want to burn
To be the darkest fire
To give the world
Everything
It doesn't get
Its countless rainbow shades

A wind howls
At the edge of the world
I sense it
I can actually see it move
Through the air
I go where no one else goes
And I live to tell the tale

The tale of the Night
Is told around campfires
Of the darkest flame
I keep howling at the moon
I hear, I speak
The whispers in the wind
The voices of the dead

They are there
At the edge of the mind
They are everywhere
They are the world
The gift of winter
Makes joy burn in my heart

I stand in pitch-black darkness
In a room without walls
I stare hard
At the nothing in front of me
Making tears jump from my eyes
I stare hard
Through the Night
Through the dreary mist
Of the gray day
I stare hard enough
To make my eyes bleed
I stare long and hard
I stare…
And I see the Fire

DEAD
2006-04-23

Dead dead dead
Dead dead dead
Dead as doornails people
Of this kingdom of the dead

I finally got inspired
Walking these streets
Of meticulous boredom
In a run of the mill town
In a state of the art
Place of fear
Nothing is up for grabs
And nothing is worth having
And life hardly feels worth living

Dead are the faceless people
Of this finely grown stone
Dead dead dead
Preserved in poison
And hard-to-breathe dust

Lips are constantly moving
Yapping all day long
Never saying shit
Only the tombstones talk
In a cold fever of rain and ashes

THE SECRET DANCE OF WRITHING
2006-05-27
The 157. night in the year of no lord 12061
In the sixth year in the time of the Twilight Storm

They came from all over the land
The princes and princesses of writhing
They came from the north
With the cold wind
They came from the southern plains
With the sultry breeze
They came from the east
With the chilly draft
And they danced from the west
Drawing the moist wind

Having crossed the hills of desolation
They gathered in the valley below
The hollow ground of dust and whispers
Of hisses and snarls and portents
Of everything they had learned to fear
Everything they had been told to shun

Lithe bodies dance as they charge forward
Writhing like the tall, whispering grass
As they, young and old and all, arrive
Arrive from the four corners of the world
Moving huskily through the grass
Between the tall, swaying trees
To the Hollow at the valley's center
A place where nothing will grow
Nothing at all

Girls and men, boys and women face off
Within the circle where fear lives
The place they had been told to shun
By the noise filling their ears and minds
Until nothing but noise remained
We don't go where we want to
The noise noised incessantly
We go where others want us to go
Good boys and girls listen to the noise
To its voice and all its works

Two females, two males call to them
The writhing sticks on the ground
Dry sticks turned moist, living things
Eyeing them with their cold, merciless stare
The slimy, writhing things coil
Around the waiting, expectant bodies
A song rises from the Hollow
From the place where nothing grows
A thousand mouths giving voice
To unspeakable and horrible acts

Lizards and all the world's reptiles
Gather around the hot-blooded humans beings
In a world without voices
They give voice to the nameless
To all disgusting and reprehensible acts
So cold, they moan, so hot, they sigh
So different and so lovely
Lovely, lovely, lovely

The kings and queens of writhing
Embrace on the hard, dusty ground
Beneath their moist, soft and gasping hides
The voice of reason rises with the embers
In the valley of the thousand fires
A cold, cold voice whispers in the Void
The volcano heat of the Abyss
I walk where no one has walked before
And I recognize every little step
Every single footprint on my path

The Silent Stare

I stand in the noisy city street
Staring at the gray wall blocking my way
Silent people speak
Not really saying much
I observe them all day long
They don't speak and they don't act
They are aye-sayers on the silent stage
And hardly more than that
Mannequins merely moving their lips
With no sound of their own
Puppets not truly giving voice to anything
Except as statues being touched by nothing
But the eternal wind

I stand frozen in the noisy city street
Bits of stone falling from my statue form
My limbs are stiff, my tears are dust
There is a cave deep within me
Never seeing the light of day
Crying its bitter dust
The eternal wind is blowing
But we don't feel it
Protected by our armor
And dull, clean claws
We may walk
But we don't move

I see nothing but the gray wall
My eyes bleed and they hurt
My eyes hurt bad
I keep staring at the tall wall
I stare until my eyes bleed
There is a wall in front of me
And I'm blind as a bat
The blind bat stands there, frozen
Wearily flapping its wings
And there's a draft
A whiff of wind in my nose
I can hardly smell it
The acid scent of the sea
Through the arid stench
Of the tombstone surrounding me
But there is something there
I stare through tears turning to blood
Washing the dust away
The wall is still there
But I no longer care
I see right through it
To the forest far away
Its smell of pins and needles
Burning in my nostrils
My nostrils shivering in the coming storm
I choke, and suddenly I regain
The use of my limbs
And I can see the trees for the forest

HERE

2006-06-06
The 167. night in the year of no lord 12061
In the sixth year in the time of the Twilight Storm

Fly
The bird can fly
Fly in fire, fly in shadow
It doesn't need to fear anything
Except perhaps death
The walking death
I see a valley
A circle of fire and shadow
And I dance in its shade
On the edge of its abyss

I travel without moving
I'm always here
In this place that is not a place
In the whispering forest
In these streets of fire
Good or bad, right and wrong

I know this place
That is not a place
But a state of mind
I know it intimately
Like the back of my hand
It's not introspect at all
But a piece of the world
Unchanged by all the garbage
We're forced to endure

I travel without moving
To the deepest Abyss of Reality
And there I find humanity
Changed, but not changed
There is no right, no wrong
But truth beneath and beyond
Beyond good and evil
In a place without
Any imposed reality

I go Traveling
And I find it
At the bottom of a cave
At the top of a howling mountain
Inside a little box of horrors
In a dusty street
In a forgotten town
And the terrible slow death
Of the world is no more

ROARING FIRES

2006-06-17
The 178. night in the year of no lord 12061
In the sixth year in the time of the Twilight Storm

They light candles for the dead
Lots of tiny, tiny flames
Leaving wet pennies made from dirt
In cold, drafty and empty buildings
On a rainy and dreary day
Giant drops fall from heaven
They bury dead skin in the ground
In soil soaked in tears
Flooded by ice-cold water

They speak in solemn whispers
About the loss of a perfect man
Of how the living will envy the dead
They drown in deepest sorrow
Wallowing in their fake grief
Rejoicing in their base relief
Celebrating the fact that
The man in the ground is dead
And they're not

Black carriages are leaving the cemetery
The candles lit for the dead
The candles drown in the rain
What is all the grieving for
What is it truly for
Is it the rotting corpse
Or truly about those
Rotting while still breathing

Thunder rolls across the sky
And people huddle in their tiny huts
In their small, confined spaces
Lightning strikes twice

There is a sound
A cry in the dark
A rumble in thc ground
There is a change
In the Earth and the sky

It is late at night
And the sky is dry
The ground is warm
And no one gets wet

Slowly cooling bodies
Are displayed on
Heaps of dry wood
People make a circle
Around the bloody and torn corpses
Hands holding torches
Are raised in a final greeting
A silent salute

One man steps forward
A man with burning eyes
No, let's not light candles
For these our dearest friends
He cries in the wind
Let's light roaring fires
Because that's what they were
What they are
Let's not mourn their passage
Let's celebrate
The life of Human Beings
And stop fearing
The hot fires of the Earth

There are loud cheers
There are wild moves
Torches joining with dry wood
Becoming the mighty flame
Rising from the ashes
The ghost of the wolf
Cries in the forest

Thunder rolls across the sky
And people straighten in their vital dance
In their vast, open spaces
Lightning strikes
Yet again

Quiet Before the Storm
2006-08-25

I want humanity to drown in blood.
I want those clinging to their slavery to choke on their own filth.
I want those shocked by my words to be rocked to their core.
I want to experience a life cleansed of poison.
I want to know power without guilt.
I want to tell absolutely all slaves what they are, and I want to see
the truth in their eyes.
I see it every day.
I want to see endless fire rekindle dead eyes.
I see it every day.
I want to see houses of cards crumble.
I see it everywhere.
I see how Death has become a joke.
How Life itself has turned into a bad punch line.
I see an endless supply of puppets on a string.
I hear people call that a life.
And I see them turn deaf ears and blind eyes to the embers in
their midst.
I see water flood every street.
The wind is blowing.
I can hear its whisper in the quietest of places.
I hear it everywhere.
I awake every morning to a semblance of a life.
We all do.
Paper-dry sock puppets of tyranny.
I want upheaval.
I want the final days to come.
I want to return to the quiet darkness, the silent roar of the Night.
I want to drown in the spice of life, not merely taste it at the tip
of my tongue.
I want conformity to return to the non-existence it is.
I want complacency and any mundane existence to end up
On the garbage heap where it belongs.
I know no mercy, no pity.
I know only the pitiless wave.
And I drink from its well.

This is life.
This truth and joy beyond sensibility.
Civilized man
Go chop your head off.
I don't want much.
I just want everything.

ANTS

I can feel the ants again
I can feel them crawling
Under my skin
In my veins
No, this is not
A drug withdrawal anxiety attack
But the silent horror
Of a million eager ants
Doing their designated job
Of servitude and frantic pacing

The eager beavers
Keep digging through my brain
As if they were born to it
They follow the orders
Of the central processing unit
Not once stopping in their tracks
Thinking about, considering
What they are doing
To me and others, to themselves
To everybody walking this Earth

There are those claiming
That current human society
Is not emulating the ants
But we clearly do that
The evidence evident
Everywhere we look
Take pieces of nature
Distort it, play it back and forth
Apply it where it
Never should have been applied
It works
You're the queen of the hill

So, here we are
Humans pretending to be ants
Pretending to be anything
Except human beings
So, where does that leave us
The great pretenders
Picture this in your mind
A poisonous, desolate place
We only glimpsed in Nightmare
Take a look at the ruins surrounding us
And you see it everywhere
This is the world
The Pretenders have made

Summer of '06
2006-09-15

It began early
Like a slow moving train
Puffing up a steep slope
It ended somewhere
In the desert sand

Heat rises from
From the sizzling city streets
Boiling the poor souls
Walking and stumbling here
Sunlight reaches
Even the deepest shadow
People glance uneasily
At each other
Between the coughs
And the gasps
Never truly looking
At themselves
In the mirror

They glimpse
Their indistinct images
In the incomplete
Store window mirror
And dream in a haze
Of poison and mirages
Of desperate imagination

And thus they keep dreaming
Their insane dreams
While the world
Goes from bad to worse
Around them

Trinkets please these people
Mirages please them
While they dance
Their fake dance
Going out of their way
To avoid dancing
Avoid living
As happiness eludes them
As life itself
Keep slipping away

It was the summer of '06
Everything happened
Everything bad and good
Now and then

The summer of '06 began early
In the unease of people's mind
And in the never ending
Desert of the world
It's still there

Taken
2006-09-26

It's spring
The scent of life
Is in the air
It's fall
The scent of death
Lingers in my nostrils
I walk down a familiar street
And I wish I was somewhere else

She breathes in the stale city air
Shrinking a bit
As she opens the window
Hammered by the noise
Assaulting her
There is a sting of pain
As she's attempting to breathe

The desert walk
Starts early in the morning
Ends late at night
Never ending
A slumbering rest
A brief respite
Is filled with dreams of relief
Potent desires of flight
Waves of distant rumblings
A rush of fresh air
In the morning.

They seek into the night
Into the deep places
That is everywhere
Also in the stone desert
Even in the stone desert
There is an elevation of spirit
An elevation of despair
There is always despair
They meet at midnight
Seeking the fire of the world
Seeking the thousand embers
The thousand treasures
Not treasures
Hidden in the dark edges
Of existence

Jenny opens the window
She opens the window
She opens the window again
And again and again and again
Breathing in poisonous fumes
Stumbling into dark alleys
And hallways
Paths not taken

They stare at each other
These hungry souls
Walking the world
With burning eyes
Recognizing the starvation
In the others' eyes

In every little gesture
And move they make
Like seeks like even more
In this world of
Phenomena and superficiality
Of trinkets and golden dragons

Something happened
In a single breath
Or during a long night
Of the soul
They were being whisked away
They were taken
Taken by their desires
Their longing and yearnings
We go where we want to go
And the world is changed
Before our senses

It's summer
The scent of life
Simmers in the air
It's winter
The scent of death
Rips through my being

The stars has fallen
The Earth has cracked in two
And everything is okay
With the world

High Tide
2006-10-26

There is a high tide tonight
And when there is
A high tide these days
It gets really high
Waves crush the shore
Turning everything to dust

I walk through the harbor
A dark, steamy night
White waves shower my body
Gushes of dust heat my soul
I visit the local tavern
A shady pearl in the ebony air
I smell the stench of malt whiskey
In the wind
I grin in expectation
In wild abandon
I wanna drown my joy
In a barrel of beer

There is no rain
Only air dry enough
To burn our lungs
We race along the intersection
Between the land and the sea
There is a high tide
And we breathe it
In gulps of fresh air

Pain cuts the world
Pain so pervasive
It makes ashes of us all
But the sorcerer
Stands on the corner
Weaving his great Chaos
Strands of night and fire
Grow out of thin air
Lightning scorches the ground

So… we sit here
At the Red Shadow Inn
Drowning our joy in beer
There is low, penetrating music
There are whispers
Haunting our ears

We sit at our corner table
Swinging our glasses
Singing our song
«I wanna drown my joy
In a barrel of beer»

DANCE, MYSTIC DANCE
2006-11-02

A breeze plays the strings
Of the forest
Shadows beat the drums
On the soft ground
In the midnight moonlight
Oozing fires strike the chord
Of sweaty bodies
Girls and boys dance
In the woods
Dance mystic dance

There is no reason here
In the swirling mist
Only all the reason
In the world
There is no passion here
In the swinging hips
Only all the sweat
In existence
Witches dance
And weave their spell
Creating the world

Singing and chanting they play
The strings of the forest
Their shadows whirl the silver light
They are dragons
Spitting oozing fires
Into the vast, putrid night
Merry witches dance
Dance mystic dance
Breathing the breath
Of the eternal forest

Dreaming are the witches
Dreaming the world
Its pleasure, joy
And endless nightmares
Vast is existence
Sad is the Universe
Dancing its merry dance
Tears drown the smiling faces
And the burning eyes
Witnessing the birth
Of everything
Being born hurts

NIGHTFALL
January 2006 - February 2007

A warm and sunny morning
I turn my head and cast my eyes back
To the black, hard surface on the ground
In the light of day it casts only
A bleak shadow haunting my dreams
The comforting day play nice in my ears
Laying my guts to rest

The wind is blowing
And I don't feel it
The wind takes hold of my hair
But it doesn't rise on my head
I walk the warm, sunny places
And I die in my sleep

But there is another world out there
I know that, in the place
The pleasant, horrible daylight
Doesn't shine

I walk the wilderness
My house is being blown to pieces in the Storm
And it creates a warm, fuzzy feeling in my gut
I take a stroll down the shadowy path
I see a ghostly light in the window
On a dry and warm night
There is a revenant howling
Where the crossroads meet

I feel a skeleton hand reach for me
In the dead of night
The bony fingers cut me open
Like flesh bleeding to death
I look behind me
I see the gray,
still photography of normalcy
I cast my vision ahead
There is the black and hard surface
I often see in my dreams

I dive beneath that black and hard surface
Breaking that black and hard surface
Breaking it in a thousand pieces
Digging in the mud,
Bathing in the molten sea
Of the cold, hard world

My shell is being torn apart
In the shrapnel wind
Laying bare the softness beneath
I embrace this change
This destruction of normalcy
Nightfall comes Calling
Breaking open the soft veil
Keeping me from breathing

I AM
I am Nightfall
I tear apart the soft veil
Keeping the Human Being
From breathing
From breathing deep and hard
From knowing the world

I run long and hard
The shadowy path of the night
A ghostly shadow appears
In my line of vision
I catch it with my eye
Holding on to it
For my dear life
There is a revenant
Howling from the Crossroads

There is dusk
There is night
A sense of life seems to be
Embracing us at Nightfall
A deep, deep hole
Swallowing us whole
And the next, next day
When it swallows the world
The revenants are
Howling from the Crossroads

THE SOFT DECEMBER RAIN
December 2006 - February 2007

I stand nude on the balcony
Staring at the soft December rain
Each drop hitting my skin
Makes it tingle and burn
Water drowns my eyes
And I see better than I ever have

What I feel is beyond excitement
Beyond any experience of the senses
What words may describe
Deeper than any ocean
I have ever known
What lay ahead of me
Is the total unknown
What I know better
Than the back of my hand

The rain is pouring
Into the sea below
Making it rise
Flooding all shores
And every single river
In existence

The sea is boiling
Hot and steamy
There is no bridge there
No horizon, no air, no sky
Only the vast, boiling sea

I stand in its midst
With the arms
Stretched above my head
I boil as it boils
I cry as it cries
I slip on its icy surface
I bath in its hot embrace
In its glowing furnace
I find myself

NOTHING HAPPENED - a ballad
2007-02-11

1.

People wonder about Jesus of Nazareth
The man they call Christ
They claim an omnipotent God
Came to Earth
And walked the land as a man
They say a weird, obscure creature
Split itself in three
In a complex scheme to save humanity
From a sin it had instigated and desired
The creature knows everything there is to know
It knows the beginning, end and new beginning
And it's bored beyond imagining

So, it put its great game in motion
Creating reality and its chess pieces
Of gold and silver and blood and bones
Its game of sin and redemption
And worship and endless trust
Or so they say

In the year zero it sent itself
To suffer on its own behalf
Creating quite the spectacle of it
A theater production
Worth its value in gold
And blood, sweat and tears
Or so they say

There are countless ancient stories
About people rising from their death
Stories about human beings
Rising from their own ashes
About humanity living on
After death

These were the stories the men of Nicaea
Breathed on and gave life
To suit their own, petty purposes
To make themselves shine
In a posterity of their own making
Many a critical scholar
Of their present
Spoke up against their lies
And many a critic's shadow
Was drowned in blood
That's the nature of religion
Anyone it can't convert
It kills

And thus it was
Through centuries and millennia
Through days and nights without number
Of deceit and horror beyond imagining
Until Jesus the mirage had become fact
Until reality itself
Had become muddled in smoke and mirrors
And Freedom a four-letter word

2

There was no man called Jesus Christ
He was and is a sick deception
Created from scratch
By people thriving on such things
On the collective insanity
Claiming the world

Nothing happened in the year Zero
Except the flow of history
The invention, the stories gone bad
They came later, centuries beyond
While power hungry old men gathered
And concocted the fraud
The utter, deluded fantasy
Deceiving and destroying the world

So, here we are today
Living without a clue
Of what the world truly is
Because of a bunch
Of power hungry old men
Claiming both their present
And posterity
As their very own
Time and countless lies
Created the legend
The pure myth of Jesus of Nazareth
And we are all worse off because of it

There is no God, no savior
Gathering the worthy
At Judgment Day
And we are all better off
Because of that jubilant fact

GOD IS DEAD (and I killed It)
2007-02-19

It began as a seed
In the mind of a boy
He saw the world
Its true nature
Far from what they told him
It was like
The seed was skepticism
And its bloom was freedom

I looked around me
I saw what the world IS
It isn't difficult
Not difficult at all
The power of observation
Of personal experience
Its basic needs
Is in us all

And as we open ourselves
Open ourselves up
To the world
As we are born
A thousand times
We open ourselves
Cutting off the cancer
The prejudice and intolerance
And disbelief instigated in us
From an early age

I saw the world as it is
I saw myself
My infinite Self
And I saw everything
God is redundant at best
To be kind
As we grow confident and wise
We leave behind the serfdom
Of religion

I killed God in myself
And thus I killed It everywhere
I removed It from the Universe
With a scalpel
Of dreams and reason

CEMETERY DANCE
2007-03-14

Corpses in the ground
Writhe their crooked dance
With a happy grin on their face
I stumble into the cemetery
By the hangman's tree

The ground is silent in my ears
There is no movement in my eyes
But the cold trickle down my spine
Is buzzing like hell in my mind

I strain my eyes
I listen until my ears hurt
I see and hear nothing
Cold sweat is condensing on my brow

Happy dance, they sing
Happy dance, happy dance
Chop his head off
Happy dance

I stop by the hangman's tree
My bloated tongue
Sticking out from my mouth
Has the color of red and blue
My body turns round and round
And the rotting corpses sing
Happy dance, happy dance

THANK YOU FOR NOTHING
2007-03-15

They tell us this is the best
Of all possible worlds
«There are problems, sure», they say
«But we're solving them
There are snags
(A lot of snags)»
They snicker
«We're picking them off
One by one»

They say this is a good life
That we shouldn't complain
That we don't have the right
That we should be grateful
For the crumbs we receive
From Life's table

They say we should be grateful
For the riches they bestow upon us
We should thank them
For the injustice, oppression
Tyranny, starvation, brutality
Dominating the world

Thank you, esteemed leader
Stinking rich fat man
Thank you for nothing
Because, in truth
Nothing is all
You've ever given us
And everything is what
You're taking away

A MEETING IN THE FOREST
2007-03-20

We meet in the forest
A bout of strangers
Joining the circle
Around the fire

There is a flow
We feel it
An uninterrupted flow
A sense of belonging
Undeniable

I enter the forest at dusk
Leaving the emptiness behind

I remember passing
A naked hill
Of chopped-down trees
Fearing the forest was shrinking

I remember imagining
The fire in the forest
And there I was
Joining the circle
Around the fire

TIRED
2007-03-23

1.

I know tired
I know it in my bones
In my bones of bones
It's not physical fatigue
But one of the gray matters
Of the spirit

I know tired
It's not a kick in the head
It's not a blow to my chest
But a thousand soft
Assaults on my very being

I know fire
I know Shadow
Beyond tired
Beyond exhaustion
I know the burning inside
Making it all worth it

2.

Daily life today
So dead, so sick
A thousand invisible hammers
In my gut
Making it hard
So hard
To breathe

It's not «worth it»
Not by any stretch
Of the imagination
But it's tolerable
We can take it
Because the burning inside
WILL transform the world

Even in the bleakest
Of circumstances
A thousand hawks
Will flap their wings
Blowing away all fatigue
Burning away everything
But the essentials
The Human Being exposed
And «tired» is only a word

THE MAN PHOTOGRAPHING A MANHOLE
2007-03-25

A man stops on a spot
In the busy harbor
A hot spring morning
He carries a camera
Around his neck

He bends forward
With his instrument drawn
Focusing on the intricate patterns
Of the manhole

What is it he sees there, I wonder
Is he attempting to solve
The many mysteries of existence
Or obscuring them to no end
In his own, befuddled mind

He snaps his slices of reality
Bending forward until his back hurts
He focuses on the circle drawn
Until his eyes turn sore

For whatever reason
He keeps studying the manhole
The manhole by his wobbly feet
Day turns to dusk, turns to night
Night turns to dawn, turns to day
The man stays his course

GHOST TOWN

1 - The tombstone dream

I walk through streets of specters
Passing puppets with empty eyes
On the sidewalk
There is no one alive
In this ghost town
This tombstone dream

There is life here, somewhere
Concealed in corners and pits
In this place of dead souls
Noise hammers us from all sides
Noise is the sound of death
Above and below, left and right
Back, front and center

Ghosts howl and wail
They bow their heads
Releasing their banshee cry
There is no fire there
The whimper is of a despair
Lacking even the slightest bit
Of messy desperation

2 - The woman at the cemetery

A woman stumbles between the tombstones
With a sword in her gut
Her blood coloring the grass
Memory fails her
As she blinks
And recalls yesterday
Recalls today and tomorrow

City streets flash
Before her weary eyes
A man points his gun at her
She draws her sword
And in one swift move
She cuts off his arm
The hot metal gun
Hits the ground
With a dump noise

In the memory of yesterday
She sees tomorrow
In the searing pain of the present
She sees yesterday
She grins and stumbles on
In one, swift move she draws her sword
And rushes on
In the memory of today
She sees tomorrow

Mist, fire and moon
2007-05-01

I lit my fire in the mist
In the low clouds surrounding the mountain
The gray, swirling mass
Drifting in from the sea
The deep, murky sea
The dancing fire grows
Reaching into the moist air
Into the silver moonlight
In the warm and humid night

One pair of feet moves
On the solid and tricky ground
Moving sideways, rotating counterclockwise
Whirling up a storm
Rhythm rises from feet
Chants rise from throat
Casting spells of mist, fire and moon
This is a special night
One where one pair of feet
Becomes many
One where a chant
Becomes a choir

The witch moves, moves feet
Moves the air, fire and mist
The swirling mist itself
The moon dances like the body does
Like the mist and fire do
Making the night breathe
Making the forest speak
Making the mountain cry out
In a piercing howl

This is the night of our ancestors
This is the night of our descendants
This is our night
Freedom from slavery
Free of any constraints
Unfettered everything
Await us in the swirling mist

I rise above the mist
Into the brilliance
Of the full moon
I dive into the mist
Pulled by the call
Of the dancing fire
Burning in the mist

Chopping wood
2007-06-19

I'm chopping wood all day
I don't see the forest for the trees
There's a big heap there
Right in front of me
And it isn't getting any smaller
No matter what I do
It stays the same

I use a big axe
A small axe
A tiny axe
Big or small chainsaws
A selection of
Electric chainsaws
It's no use
It stays the same

That's chopping wood for you
An exercise in futility
The heat grows and you shrink
And not all the tools in the world
Can help you

I use friggin dynamite
I use controlled demolition
I blow it all to Kingdom Come
I detonate a nuclear bomb
I bleed a waterfall of tears
In friggin frustration
The heap of wood stays the same

I die there, on the bed of chopped wood
Never even seeing or glimpsing
The top of the heap

I slice my bread with a dull knife
2007-06-09

A trumpet is triumphing its way
Through the forest
Slicing and dicing like hell
Screams and horrors
Of infinite magnitude and quality
Follow in its metal steps
Its triumphant song
Shivering between the trees
I slice my bread with a dull knife

Boots are stomping city ground
Making and shaking the poison juice
There is an ongoing march
The city dwellers know well
One stomping everyone and everything
Boots kick their heads
Boots kick their ass
Their insane trumpet
Reverberating through sore ears
I slice my bread with a dull knife

Promises of spring

They claim that autumn has come
Incredible as it sounds
That's what they say
They stare through the window
In the searing heat
And feel cold flow through the veins

I say, like I have been saying for a while
That spring is well under way
That we can see it bloom
That its distant thunder
Is in the very air we breathe

In the whirlwind we see ourselves
Our terrifying Self
Through the window we stare at
All the fabulous we fear
And fear comes with spring
The Thunder Road is waiting
Around the next turn

The boiling water is drowning us
Tearing the flesh from our bones
The dry sand and wind
Make it hard to breathe
Lightning splinters the mist blinding us
Thunder comes with the warm wind

Desert voice
2007-08-05

The night is quiet
We can hear the grains of sand
Rub against each other
In the shadows
But the desert is quiet
A silence we have never before
Been listening to
Except in our deepest Self

It's such a short stretch out here
Just a few steps
And we are here
We are here in the whirlwind
Listening to the desert voice

The grains of sand rub
Against each other
And the desert speaks to us
We hear the souls of the dead
Only in the silence out here
We can hear ourselves speak.

I HEARD A RAVEN
2007-10-18

I heard a raven
Its dark, lovely cry
Somewhere to the left
I heard the flapping of wings
And I saw the echoes spread
In the early twilight air

I walked past a tree
On a branch I imagined
I saw a raven

The streets are silent
In my ears
I hear all the sounds
I want to hear
The light is gone
From my eyes
I see all the sights
I want to see

I stopped before a tree
Even as I kept walking
In this rare moment of time
The traveler halts
In his tracks
And ponders
Ponders deeply the world
And on the lower branch
Of the tree
I see the raven
Forever More

THE MOON IS SHINING
2007-11-11

The moon is shining
From a cloudy sky
The valley is covered in mist
And the moon is obscured
In a transparent veil of tears
But walk to the mountain top
And you discover the truth
The moon needs no sun to shine

The moon is shining
So pale in the night sky
So much brighter than the star
At the other side of exciting dusk
Shadow is growing
In the brightest of spots
In valleys, forests and on mountains
Life and fire, fangs and claws
Travel into the night
Reaching into the most intense
Piece of the human heart

Covered in mist and shadow
The human beings need no light
To show them the way

WHAT IS WHAT
2007-12-02

I know what is what
Even though it can be hard sometimes
I know what life is
Even though it can be hard
To see sometimes
Glimpsed through layers upon layers
Of poisonous mist

We're all living in a brothel
Filled with prostitutes and convicts
And there is no way out
It might be pleasant enough
With soft beds and silken sheets
There may be no bars
Covering our windows
But we're still living in a cell

They say we should think positive
We shouldn't shake the bars
And we should smile
To the men and women in uniform
Patrolling the prison yard
Smile as we are brought
On our daily walk
As they pull the leash fastened
To the collar around our neck

Our masters are kind
They give us plenty of fresh air
As it is
They want what's best for us
For what it's worth

I know what's what
Although it can be confusing
Sometimes
How can it not
In a world of the clearest air
With all its fog
Filling our head

FALLING
2008-03-06

I saw her falling
Bright as day
On the blackest night
I watched as her form
Hit the wet ground
Cracking open like an eggshell
The shadow, her shadow
Dark and potent
Revealed itself to me

She, she walked
Down the street
The shadowy street
With me
Flashing her fangs
The hellish creature
The beyond lovely
Beast of flesh and fire
Looked at me
And revealed her fangs

I saw her rising
Black as night
On the brightest day
I beheld her Shadow
The Sun in the sky
And the darkest
Most delicious thoughts
Filled my mind

We are falling
Through intricate space
Forever falling
Until damning words
Have meaning no longer
We flow through
The black velvet sky
Born in that
Eternal living sea
With murder and mayhem
On our mind

Shallow ground

I wanted to call this poem «a poem without a title», but I changed my mind.

Distant thunder rolls towards you
Beneath the shallow ground
Trees shake in expectation
Leaves dance in the quiet air

Shadows dance in the wall of clouds
Smiling to you
Grumbling at you
Under the wide brimmed hat

Flashes darken the road you walk
They blink and greet you
They jump and sway
Crushing you to dust

Dust quivers in the quiet air
Above the shallow ground
They sing with their red lips
They cackle with their hoarse voice

Your feet smile
Your sore head tramps
The soft soil
Wearing out weary soles

Quivering the shallow ground

Running through the night
2008-04-17

I hear a whisper
A hiss in the wind
In the city of many ghosts
I run afoul the mysteries of life
I get a dose of full blown reality
As the coach and horses
Are seen, heard and felt

It is coming from nowhere
Going nowhere
Bewildered people hear its cry
There is nothing there
Nothing they can grab
Or hold on to
No bricks or mortar
Or solid sound
Only a whisper
A hiss in the night
In the eternal twilight
In the city of many ghosts

Under a violet moon
Between castles and dreams
There is a dance
A whirl of the ages
Hooves hammer at the ground
Misty burning wheels keep turning
Throwing sparks of darkness
Into the brightest day
As the coach keeps looking
For something he may never find

My feet stop moving
And my body freezes
Standing there unmoving
As I raise my head
And sniff the scent in the wind

I can hear the coach and horses
Run through the night

This moment
2009-01-31

I'll remember this moment
This bursting ember in time
Like an endless row
Backwards and forwards
On the invisible trail

We slay the knight
In his castle
Roasting him to
A tasty crisp

We sat around the long table
Toasting to the night
To the fire flowing
Between our lips

We are children of the sea
Playing on its wet shore
We feed on tasty meat
On great beverages
After going hungry and thirsty
For so long
for so very long

The day begins
The night doesn't end
We are children of the sea
Playing on its wet shore

I see all tomorrow's endings
Like all yesterdays' failures
The more things change,
The more they stay the same

I SLEEP
2009-03-09

I sleep
These days
Imagining
My hibernation dreams
Writing these nights
Of mist and shadow

Wake up, human being, wake up
From your slumber and your death
Go where you haven't gone before
And see for yourself
What life is like

We need your dark tonight
There is a song hummed
By the motley crew
Traveling through the night
We need your dark tonight
Just need, beyond needing
To share your dark tonight
The release of your dark passions
Tonight

There are so few of us
So few shouting
In the night
We are waiting for you
Out there
On the mighty Shadow's wave

And awake is the dream
And sleep is the reality
The truth nagging my buds
Writing these nights
Of mist and shadow

Two poems of fire and ashes

Boiling waters
2009-06-20

We saw the three girls
Stand on the sidewalk
Across the street
Caught in a cage
Their claw-like fingers
Clutching the bars

We stood on our side
On our sidewalk
Caught in a cage
Our claw-like fingers
Clutching the bars
We glimpsed ourselves
In the hazy window

We swim through boiling waters
At the heart of Life's Fire
Long and dark shadows
Are cast in ancient hallways
Shadows flicker wherever
Our attention turns

We see the girls through the bars
Or is that they seeing us
Day turns to night
And night becomes the life it is
The bullies in uniform
Fade away to nothing
To the insignificance they are
It isn't us seeing the bars
And it isn't the girls
At the heart of Life's fire
There are no such sick things

BORN FREE
2009-05-20

Born free
Growing up in chains
And behind bars
This is today's
Undeniable state of mankind

This is a fact
A horrible truth
In a society
Based on lies and deceit
A destructive illusion
Of the first order

Children
Born to be free
Grow up in prison
Never truly growing up
At all
A true hell
With no exits
Children
Born to be true
Never growing up at all
Sheep grassing in the field
Puppets dancing in strings
Dying of old age
Still young
Never asking the right questions
Or seeking the right answers

Born free
Into an insane world
Collared and chained
Believing this is how
It's supposed to be
Look at anyone today
And that's what you'll see

The misty and chilly night

Misty fog in the night
The best of two worlds
Clarity beyond words
A glimpse of a shadow
In the dark window
Five seconds
And everything opens up
Indefinitely

A chill down the spine
A touch of The Other World
Of potential unleashed
Of humanity incarnated

I walk the forest at night
I'm doing it right now
In tracks of blood and dirt
And imagination unbound

In the cemetery the dead rose and left
And it was a cemetery no more
But a forest
No longer a nice cut lawn

Setting loose the Storm

2009-05-20 - 2009-08-30

It's just a tiny flap of wings at first
I sense it on the edge of my vision
In a shade of green in the green
It's there, no doubt about it
Right before my eyes and hands
So powerful, like a shiver in the ground

It's just such a tiny flap of wings
Compared to the onslaught of civilization
Deadly and horrible, surrounding us
It's just an ant carrying a leaf
A river flooding the nearest fields
Everything is seemingly so peaceful

The mighty city spreads from a single point
Strangling the land, the very life on Earth
Tall tombstones rise to rival the sky
Human beings suffer and die far below
The mighty city is destroying
Everything making life worth living

Life itself is choked by its poisonous breath

The city dwellers walk back and forth in a daze
They gaze at the world through a dirty haze
Everything that moves, lives and dreams
Is captured behind the dead beast's bars
The Machine roars, and the two-legged mouse whimpers
Moving like puppets in strings and chains

Factories and pipes spit deadly poison
Turning the air deadly to breathe
Turning the water deadly to drink
Turning the soil deadly to touch
All are well with the world, they say
The puppet masters, the many-headed beast
Ruling the world

The Machine has taken over the world
Fooling mankind into thinking they are in charge
The Machine is vast, vast as the world
Many people believe it is the world
Unstoppable, mighty beyond nature
Beyond anything remotely human

I've lived a lie of my own choosing
I've lived a lie burying my Self
I've hidden the world from myself
But now i know what I've forgotten
Now I know what I've always known
I know what the modern world is
I know it must be destroyed

Everybody knows in their heart
That civilization itself
Must be destroyed beyond salvaging
This is hard but not impossible
It's just a machine, man-made
And certainly vulnerable

Soft and brittle beneath its thin skin

One butterfly emerges from its chrysalis
Flaps its wings, shouting in the wilderness
A river is flooding its nearest fields
A rock hits the water, creating its rings
The rings don't weaken, but grow in strength
A tall building shakes in the wind

On the place of dry, dry trees
The drying wind blows, spreading
Spreading across fields and seas
Making all things brittle and parched
I feel the wind of change
The wind of change blowing wild

The restless air, the boiling seas
Are surging through red blood
All the red blood there is
At the heart of the dead world

Releasing what is already free

Wild growth supplants
The world that was
This is The Twilight Storm
These are the final days

Sorcerer
2009-10-16

I tear at the skin of life,
and breathe its dust,
its ashes of the coming fire
I pick sounds formed like words
from the autumn air,
and I speak the Magick
of the rotting leaves
and temporary death

I tear off flesh to the bone
And taste its blood
Its tainted oxygen,
its lifeless water
I spot pictures dull like paintings
From the castle's dusty hall
And I see the sorcery
of the ancient walls
and innoculus life

During the three years of mighty flight
I learned to read truth on pieces of skin
In bowls of blood and dry bones cast to the ground
I learned to see in the dark, to hear it move
In the swift flash of a black blade
I saw the rainbow shadow of the world

All Soul's Night
Late October/early November 2009

I see masks dance in the air
I see them fall like rain
On All Soul's Night

I see the weird shimmer in the night
Something different from what my eyes see
Everything is opening up
On All Soul's Night

A woman is coming at me from the left
I see beyond her mask
To her seething Shadow beyond
Boiling blood flows through my veins

I died the first time when I was three
Floating under the ceiling
Looking down on my blue, still body
Listening to people speak far away
Breaking through the veil
To the Other World

I returned from a land
Of mist and shadow
So much more
Than I had been

I died the second time
When i was nine and a score
I fell on my back
And as my worried friends
Gathered around my still body
I fell into a hole black and deep
To The Other World

I saw so much more this time
Of the land of mist and shadow
I sensed spirits, ghouls and
What was Beyond
Knowing my distant friends
And the world they roamed
Better than I ever had
In an instant or two or three
During the time I was dead
Everything woke up inside me

And it stayed awake, stayed open
Like it does to this day
On this All Soul's Night

In a glimpse, in a mirror
Far more powerful than the reflection
We see ourselves as we truly are

The savage
2009-12-04

A man is chanting
On a street corner
Outside my window
The chant is vibrating
The air and ground
Spreading far and beyond
Its humble origins

Wild, ancient power
Is present in that sound
In that Human Being
Standing there with
Outstretched arms

He is clearly a savage
Wearing modern garbs
Not a religious nut
Praising his god

I stand there transfixed
In his presence
Enjoying the heat
Of his fire
The closeness of
His fire and passion

He is not outside my window
Not in front of me anymore
But I am, there, ahead
Attracting other humans
With my song

A rose and thorns
2009-12-04

There was a rose and there were thorns
In my path
I love to see her bloom
I don't mind stabbing myself
On thorns now and then
Don't mind them piercing my skin
And draw a few drops of blood

On the invisible path of night
We indulge in our dark passions
On freedom unbound
Liberated from ridiculous
And horrible confinement
Imposed by the light of day
And a society without a clue
What a Human Being is

The maid found the hotel room
Filled with body juices
On walls, sheets and floor
And even the ceiling
The scents assaulting her senses

Others have reason to envy us
The night girl tells me across the table
Over steaming hot coffee
Envy our soaring emotions
The place in ourselves
Where we leave nothing behind

I certainly agree
As I feel the thorns
Pierce my skin
As the scent of the rose
Burns so pleasantly
In my nose

When I close my eyes
And see the streets of London
It's her I see in my mind
It's her scent I smell
In the wind
Her blood I taste
On my tongue
The wild forests of London
Stay fresh in my memory

As I know beyond knowing
We'll meet again

Forever Euphoria
2010-03-03

Windy is the night
Quiet is the light
Lavender soft
Is the calm storm

The big girl sings with the choir
Of the wretched church
She chants with the warm, warm rain
Flowing like the river
In the sizzling, naked spring

Dark is the wind
Hot is the blood
Stark is the draft
From the shadows
From the corners
Of the wild Earth

The wilderness snarls in joy
Before the looking glass ahead
Fangs and claws of the Earth flash
In the darkness beyond the tiny lamp
In the delicious soup enhancing
The great taste in your mouth

From the belly it's spreading
To body and mind
The euphoria of life
Unbalanced fire
Forever and ever yours

Death and remembrance
2010-05-31

I remember a time of strife
And the death of spirit
Of rotting spirits in heaps
Of blood frozen in veins
Of life itself fading

I turned forward in my tracks
And saw another world
Of soaring spirits in crowds
Of blood flowing in veins
Of life itself reborn

Taking a good, hard look at the world yesterday
Was like watching death of spirit incarnated
Like seeing everything making life worth living
Fading away into the nothingness of non-existence
Fifty birds with one stone, and we were all gone

I remember it all, the time of strife
The turnaround, the reawakening of spirit
The return of the Human Being
Reborn in blood, boiling in the veins
Still, to this day, these lovely long nights
Of freedom and joy and wild abandon
Death and remembrance haunt us
Like a distant echo in the horizon left behind

Under a Hollow Moon
2010-08-27

I do ask myself sometimes
If it's worth it
I guess everybody does
In their grayest of moments

I rise from my grave of day
When the beasts of night
Roam the savage, desolate Earth
And rediscover what's lost

In the Hollow Moon inside
Where most people today
tragically fear to tread
I find my treasures

Under the Hollow Moon
In what is misplaced today
I find everything valuable
In a Human Being

Bird of Prey
2010-11-01

Vibrations of guitar strings
On the Underground
The underground of humanity
Haunting notions of life unbound

A bird charged me
And missed by a notch
Every time a bird has
Missed me like that
Death has touched me
Its wings flapping
At my outer limits

I sit by the open door
In beautiful November
And there is no draft
I love how dishes
From all over the world
Are available all over the world
Everything opens up
With each new breath
Meal, taste, smell and touch

The necromancer
The animator of dead souls
Reaps the whirlwind
Of the wide-open door

On the day of the dead
Death touched me
Rocks rolled down
The ever-lasting slope

The Book of the Dead
Opened its pages to us
Two pinpricks in eternity
Told their story

The bird of prey
Is flapping its wings
The human fire
Is burning in my gut

The dry wind
2010-12-18

The dry wind is blowing
Drying everything
The door is wide open
The music is loud and wild
In the distance, beyond the noise
The thousand year wind is roaring

Something is hidden in the streets
Of civilized, modern humanity
Right there, at the edge
Of the blind, narrow-chinked eye
Rests concealed, misplaced
The mystery of us all

The dry wind comes a'calling
Destined to blow a thousand years
Hard and relentless it blows
Rocking humanity to the core
In the distance, beyond the noise
Everything forgotten and misplaced
Is exposed

Just off the next corner
Or the corner just passed
Beyond the ridiculous concern
Of routine and false duty
A thought long gone
Manifests yet again

Flesh is ripped off bone
In a hurricane of fire
An irresistible flood of thought
We find what's missing
From our wretched life
We discover what's lost

Words
Written in 2 minutes by the Stunt Poet 2011-02-27

It isn't the words
But the reality behind them
Behind the words
Of longing
Passion
And the fire and night
Of the Universe

The Rainbow Path
Dreamed in twilight
The Path of the Witch
Of the Human Being
Incarnated

The eyes of the Wanderer
Looking at everything
From every angle
Big and small

These are words
These are fire and night
These are Life
From angles
Too many to count

Days of long shadows
2011-11-03

We open our eyes
It's a strange sensation
Almost beyond the body
We find ourselves
In far away places
We tell the stories about
Days of long shadows
Creating ourselves from nothing

We meet at the way station
Under the Ogala tree
Pondering our burning thoughts
And enjoying a perpetual
State of being both
During the days of the long shadows
We're all Changed

We *feel*
Burning with awareness
Spices fall from the tree
And we catch every piece
Within and right beyond our grasp
Reaching as we ever do
For distant shores

I spot the girl with glowing eyes
I know her breath,
Her voice and dark passions
They are mine, not mine
The whirl of motion
Called human beings
Leaves the Ogala tree
Carrying it with us wherever we go

The sun casts its shadows
At a low and odd angle
Autumn announced its presence
Muted and distant
Far less real than the summer
We left behind
The long, bright night has come
During the days of long shadows
We're all transformed

Home
2011-12-06

The dark forest we walk
Has a white sheet
It is quiet these nights
Yet teeming with life
We can hear without effort
The fire down below

We pass through a cemetery
Striving to breathe
In its atmosphere
Of poison fumes
An unhealthy mist
Lit by a thousand dirty lights
It's just a bad memory in gray
We quickly leave behind

The dark, dark forest we walk
On its bed sometimes white
Sometimes brown and green
We breathe a sigh of relief
We have returned *home*

Spell of empowerment
2011-12-22

I Free myself from the illusion
Of light and dark, good and evil
From wretched duality
I am free to further liberate myself
To embrace the rainbow
Of Fire and Life
The Shadow that is our eternal Self

I seek other venues, other worlds
This world as it truly is
I venture into the deepest night
And find other bright shadows
I reject the horrible society
Of this day and age
And its illusions and oppression
Its existence hostile to all Life

I know what I am, now
I have known for a long time
I draw to me all knowledge
To push me further on my quest
To embrace the night and its true life
The Moon casting many and deep shadows
Teaching me to be Human
Not a robot of the Machine
Poisoning our body and spirit
Lessening the world

I free myself every day
From the web of death becoming chains
Each morning we forget little by little
What the Night taught us
What it whispered and roared
From our deepest core
I embrace the night
And also the true dawn
Waiting for us somewhere ahead
When the Machine of gray daylight
Is No More

The bullies' ball

I am a boy with a certain taste
I pump iron and strike sacks
With my sore hands and strong feet
I love seeing fear in people's eyes

I played with kittens when I was a kid
They squealed and loved it
When I burned them with cigarettes
And beat them with sticks

My first girlfriend squealed in gratitude
When I showed her who is the boss
When I beat her ass sore
When I slapped her around

I am a girl with a certain taste
I pump iron and strike sacks
With my sore hands and strong feet
I love seeing fear in people's eyes

My first boyfriend
Didn't like it when it turned rough
When I tied him up
And whipped his ass

I made him cry out in joy
I made him beg for more
And gave him everything
That has become his heart's desire

I slammed punks on the street
And four-eyes in the schoolyard
Throughout my enjoyable teens
It felt good, felt so very right

I struggled with finding my place
The world didn't seem quite right
Didn't really live up to my
Expectations, you know

Today is a big day
We received our uniforms
Our blue armor
Our shields and clubs
We stand with equals
In their eyes
We see acceptance
And the thrill
Of familiarity
We have found our calling
Become police officers
Accepting the accolades
Of an admiring world

2012-01-01
With special thanks to my friend Yngve, who told me he had nothing
against police officers.
And to the great Occupy-movement, the people who have most recently
suffered most of the bully's stick.

Red ladder dancing
2012-02-08

Pairs of deep eyes
Meet across the street
Facing each other
Possibly colliding
Like motes of dust
In the gulf of Space
Red and gray mist
Shimmer in the air
In dark back alleys
In warm and cozy cellars
This is not sad fucking blues
This is red ladder dancing

Glowing in red and silver
The wretched tripod ladder
Is glowing in the dark
Open eyes see it easily
All the colors of the night
Rushing through the door ajar
Open eyes descend the stairs
To the open spaces
Welcoming the embers
Of night and fire and shadow
This is not sad fucking blues
This is red ladder dancing

A negative son of a bitch
2012-02-23

I enjoy silence
I love the quiet night
The mystery of the mist
Even bright sunshine
Holds a certain
Appeal to me

But when I face injustice
When inequality
Rears its ugly head
I am a negative
Mean, son of a bitch

When a billion factories
Poison the Earth
When humanity
Keeps destroying
The very means
Of its own survival
I'm pessimistic
Beyond words

Please, asshole
Don't call yourself
An optimist
Call yourself
An idiot, a fool
Of the first order

Long live pessimism
Negativity long live
Spit at the optimist
At such a blatant
Stuffy head

Somewhere in the deep night
In the vast wilderness
In a distant, future land
The negative son of a bitch
Gives his comrades in arms
His best smile

Jumping off the pink cloud
2012-02-23

Love isn't the answer
Spending your life on a pink cloud
Isn't the answer at all
It's merely one more illusion
Making today's fucked up world

Why is the world filled
With silly love songs?
That one is easy to answer
Those in charge
Want it like that

My contempt is boundless
For such profound bullshit
And for those buying it
Hook, line and sinker

Carefully woven illusions
Make today's world
Keeping people in
Their dreadful state of
Suspended animation
Wake up, man
And smell the stinking
Poisonous coffee

Statement
2012-02-29

The texture is so rich
The fabric feels so good
On my sensitive skin
I stand before the mirror
Admiring myself
Feeling a little silly

I don't really need
Any outward expression
Of my nature
No dark clothes
Or anything

Clothing doth not
A woman make
Doth not make me
Perhaps it would
A trollop with no
Thoughts in her head

But I look good
In black and red
And violet hue
Under the silky hood
My eyes turn
A deeper shade

I make no statement
With the clothes I wear
Whatever beauty
And depth and fancy
There might be
Comes from within
And not from
Fancy coating and paint

But I look good
In black and red
And violet deep
My skin turns
A shady hue
My dark leather boots
Feel good on my feet

Empty hallways
2012-02-29

I don't like
The sound of steps
In empty hallways
They are loud
And certainly not
Pleasant to the ear

I pace the floor
In my paltry room
In the old, worn hotel
The sound of steps
Constantly
Ringing in my ears

You would be wrong
If you believe
This is a tale
About mental problems
This is a tell tale story
About loud noise
In empty hallways

I rush to the door
I wrest it open
And peek outside
And there is
No one there

T r u t h (2012)
2012-03-28

Truth is crushed to earth
It is beaten, kicked and ignored
While it is down
Bloody and ragged
Confronted with the lie
With even obvious falsehood

Children are terrorized
And imprisoned and killed
Suffering the death of spirit
From they are very young
Adults avert their eyes
Preferring blatant propaganda
To the beyond obvious reality
Truth is crushed to earth
Bloody and dirty and down

People nod in agreement
When a president
Speaks of himself as
A friend of israel
When he speaks with apparent sincerity
About a perceived enemy
And the need to invade
Yet another nation
Not threatening anyone

You may feel that the lie
Has the upper hand today
That people's gullibility
Knows no bounds
And you may be right
But the lesson of history
Teaches us otherwise
Even if falsehood prevails
Even if the victorious
And mindless imagination
Float to the top
What really matters is
Trivialized and ignored

People know, deep down
That the lie has become the truth
No matter what the brainwashing
And bullshit propaganda says
When we open our eyes wide
There is zero distortion
I choose to be optimistic here
People will wake up and
Smell the stinking coffee
They will bury the lie
Reject the falsehood
Of those in charge
Truth crushed to earth
Will rise again
That moment is now

The dark passion path
2012-03-29

Feet walk the rarely tread crimson trail
Through a forest deep and moist and warm
In the forever twilight summer far
Eyes spot the game swift and frail
And blood fills a mouth breathing hard
Fills a body burning in need and tar

Ashes turn to fire
Saliva to spices
Bones to molten rock
Flesh to water
Burning like fire

On a night like all others
The mind racing through the forest
Reaches the pond in the glade
Hissing like the boiling blood
Flowing through its veins

The dark is shining through curtains bright and lean
On a meadow, a heath beyond the moor far and wide
The wet ebony blade marks the way elusive and slight
A path covered by pieces of flesh steaming and thick
Silence reigns in the lodge dark and loud
The mist of the mind is fading away fast and dry
The sword reaches the bush hot and sore
And everything is all right in a world swift and lax

Walking dead girl
2012-05-05

I don't know why I'm here
The young girl said
In misery and anguish
It's all such a drag, you know
I see row upon rows of trees
Through my vision hazy by happy tears

Those staring dead eyes
Haunt my every waken moment
I walk the cemeteries of the world
Bodies in heaps stink
Like yesterday's laundry
A hoarse crow squeaking

Tombstones stained in blood
Grow around me as I walk
The taste of cold vomit
Taints everything I eat
The sweet stench of dead bodies
Welcomes me as I turn the corner

Happy masks greet me
As the sun rises
Above the horizon
Beyond sad screams
Make my ears bleed
And my eyes flood
With rust and dawn

I tale a stroll down the road
Humming carefree and wild
The birds are singing my song
The wolves are joining my howl
I see row upon rows of trees
Through my vision hazy by happy tears

Tonight
2012-05-13

This is the time
This is the night
We say goodbye
To all bad things
We take one step
Into the dark
The seething world
Where we can breathe

We rush through gates
Many and deep
Finding ourselves
At a place of
Thousand shadows
Where too many
To be counted
Dark, deep passions
Rule the vast land

We didn't leave behind
Much to speak of
Only trinkets
A few pale lights
And nothing more

This is it, folks
Dear loyal friends
On this thin raft
Our moment true

I carried this
Piece of paper
In my pocket
For a long time
Nothing had been
Written on it
It was dusty
Dirty and worn
I couldn't tell
Why I hadn't
Thrown it away
Why I had not
Supplanted it
With a new and
Better model
I didn't know
Why I kept it
There by my heart
Until I grabbed
My well used pen
And magick words
Appeared in fire
Before my eyes

She bleeds like a hose
The City of Cities 2012-09-09

The homeless man
Is a cold, rigid stiff
When the police come and fetch him
The sun dried his body
During the desert-hot day
He sipped lots of water
But it was no use
His mind was as dried and used up
As his skin and bone body

Around the corner
As close as a breath
A young woman sits on her ass
Leaning against the wall
It finally dawns on some
Of those present that the
Woman crouching on the street
And looking at them
With hazy eyes
Is bleeding hard

A deep cut has opened up her belly
She makes an attempt at speaking, at screaming
But there is no sound
As blood and guts and shit
Flow from her wound
Life has left her slowly
Through many years of suffering
And now, in a burst of lightning
She's done

A man walks around the corner
Attempting to get the attention
Of the men and women in blue
«Stop pestering us»,
An officer growls
«Can't you see we're
Fucking busy here»?

The Freedom Poem
2012-09-09 – 2012-10-30

1. Youth

The marching band moves on
Like a pleasant sound
In our filled-with-wool mind
Raw, uncompromising thoughts
Fill my blazing consciousness
The mind-numbing wool long forgotten

I walked a foreign beach once
It wasn't that foreign or far away
But I felt something
Something I couldn't name
I passed a spot on a street
A spot I had passed
Many times before
A shadow crossed my eyes
A lifetime, it stretches out before me
Like an endless road
A warm trickle down my spine

I started searching
Alone and with others
For that special place
I feared I would never find

2. Belgrave Square

We went to Belgrave Square
A warm spring evening
A place and time
Resting in infamy

We saw a bird with mighty wings
Release itself from chained hands
We were those hands
We are those birds

The gathering in Belgrave Square
Brought people from across the land
Brought avid searchers from far lands
Brought us here, all the way
The long, long way to Belgrave Square

It surged through us,
the Call of the Wild
It rose like a Storm within
The mighty roar
Of our burning hearts

It changed our lives that night
Whatever had been was no more
What we had been
Before those unforgettable moments
Was no more

Freedom remains a four-letter word
In the society of our birth
But we said goodbye to all that
In a blink of an eye
Lasting forever

Belgrave Square isn't a time or place
But a state of mind without end

3. Freedom Road

The years pass by
They fly like birds
Crawl like ants
Sometimes there is quiet
Sometimes there is noise
High or low, near or far
Our racing heart keeps beating
Keeps hammering in our chest

And I want to keep shouting loud and clear
To act fierce like the great savage I am
I want to cover the world in dogshit
Making everybody smell the stench
Because there is a horrible need
One so vast it cannot be measured
For deniers to face the obvious truth
To see through the thick fog they call a mind
And see our society for the piece of shit it is

I don't ask what price
I may have paid
For my rejection
Of an ordinary life
There is no price paid
Only the joy of my gain

I'm alive out here
On the Freedom Road
On the excited walk
Begun all those years ago
At Belgrave Square

Ravens flying through Shadow (lover of the dark)
2012-12-22

The cold wind blows through me
The volcanic heat rises within
I walk on a path my eyes cannot see
The sight of the dark lodge ahead
Fills my vision in broad daylight
Pulling me harder forward
Every eager step I take

Someone whispers to me:
«Life is a raven
Flying through Shadow»
Even as I find myself nodding
Nodding in agreement
I realize startled
That I hear the sound
Of my own voice

I move through the night
It surrounds me like a glove
A pleasant glow
Making my blood boil
On a slow burn
This lover of the dark
Seeks others like herself

A park resembling a forest
Indistinct shadows turn solid
Into human beings
They want us to forget the night
To eradicate it from our consciousness
Remove it from human life altogether
And most people just blink
And just like that
Everything valuable in their life is gone
But we refuse to do that
A stubborn streak, a drive emanating
From the core of our being
Makes us hold on
With all that is left of our heart
Night people seek to
Reclaim what is lost
Reclaim the Human Being
I greet my fellow travelers
On the ebony path
Through the Sherwood Forest
We welcome each other
To the wonderful world
Beyond the wretched mirage
The Sherwood Forest isn't a place
But a state of mind

The summer of discontent
A poem, a song, a novel, a film.
2012-12-05 – 2013-02-08

I'm Lucy Diamond
The woman with dark hair
And a red diamond
Twinkling near my heart
I stack my deck, begin the beguine
Devil Darkthrone, the red-haired man
Welcomes me at the circus of light
I show him the first card, a slice of cheese
He laughs contemptuously at me, at the upstart
- Look at it, I shout. – *Look* at it!
The slice of cheese changes dramatically
Into something dark and profoundly sinister
And his arrogant laughter and superior attitude
Become an uncertain, childish giggle

I wade through the deep snow
During the long, cold winter
To reach this summer of discontent
I breach the devil's bright den
Impressing him with my card tricks
Revealing to him the queen of spades
He reaches across the table
His clawed hand grabbing my sore jaw
Telling me the sweet words I want to hear
- You're hired, little bird
I wear my high heels
A revealing skirt
And matching jacket
My breasts on proud display
We walk up and down the street
In an endless, perpetual loop
And I can't find my path
I kneel before him
Begging him to teach me the secret

I sit here in the wretched circle
Among my peers with broken wings
Looking at them with concealed contempt
They applaud me and praise me
Knowing nothing of what I am
They give me their hearts
Offering their smile and thoughts and soul
And I return nothing but my mirrors
Of dancing playful shadow fire
I do give them my piece of mind
But they don't get it, don't understand
Don't understand any of it
Don't realize the well seen subtext
The true meaning beyond the illusion
How could they, with their limited grasp of reality
I will show them the truth, I know that
Show them the subtext of the world
I will tell them all about
What the world is about

We walk the streets afterwards
Continuing our low-keyed happy talk
Exchanging addresses and lives
In rapid, breathless succession
Days and nights of summer pass by
And we keep doing all that
Like giggling, star-eyed girls
Having a blast

Devil Darkthrone, the red-haired man
Takes me under his wings
My studies begin in earnest
He challenges and prods me
Making me the creature
Of shadow and fire
I've always wanted to be
The summer of discontent finally ends
And the summer of malcontent begins

In long October nights
I learn everything
I've ever yearned to learn
On one long night
Everything beyond that
Comes to me
The blood and sacrifice drown me
And I can finally breathe
Beyond all hurdles and boundaries
Of an enclosed mind

End of waiting
2012-12-09

This is the world as I know it
And I know it well
Centuries, millennia have passed
Since I first became aware
I brush aside red curtains
And I see the world exposed
That's all there is to it

The stone walls don't matter
They no longer matter
I look through them
As if they aren't there
I touch flesh and drink its blood
I become one with
The burning of passion and mind
I consume myself
In the upheaval
Of its deep well

I'm waiting no more
I've been waiting for so long
But now I'm waiting no more
I move among equals
Among true friends
Roaming the ages

Dark Passions
2013-01-22

The human depths
Know no bounds
There is nothing
Able to halt
The expression of
Our dark passions
I love that
I love it every time
I see it expressing itself
My eyes are filled with joy
Every time I see anyone
Expressing it

This is us, this is human
Beneath beyond hollow pretense
This is the badly hidden secret
Of our existence
Our glorious life

I catch it in a glance
A woman sends me
We encounter each other
In a busy street
Against all odds
I brave the hurdle
Of my upbringing
And approach her
Asking her casually
If I can offer her
A cup of coffee

I did that the first time
In my misspent youth
And have continued doing so
In the many years following
That fateful moment
I made her scream in delight
I awoke the ravenous beast
It scratched my skin
It drank my blood
That great night lasted forever
Not ruined by the pale light
Of the approaching day

I found her and found her again
In time and time of endless night
Of perpetual dark passions
Sometimes the shaken female
Fled like a frightened dove
At the coming of dawn
But quite a few times
She didn't, didn't back off
Didn't deny her base nature
And every time that happened
Is beyond precious to me
To my dark passions

What I hate
What disgusts me
More than anything
Is the numerous displays
Of the mundane
I gawk at its
Pretense of power
I snarl at its attempts
Of relevance
I didn't before I woke up
I do it even more now
When exciting waken dreams
Fill my existence
My powerful life
Of *Fire* and *Shadow*

The Long Morning
2013-03-03

I had a long morning tonight
It lasted twelve hours
And was filled with midnight
The dance of swords began
Just after red dusk
And continued far into dawn

The day burned one hour
Bathed in the rays
Of the eternal daystar
Rivers flowed like sand
Silver rays of the moon
Lit the clouded twilight

I spot flickers of illumination
Under the flaky door
In broad daylight
I walk through the night
Cheerful and dark
Transparent and deep

The tales of the Long Winter
2013-03-03

I'm looking forward to hear more about them.
The old woman was good at telling them to the boy.
And I love that both summer and winter are long and strange
The tales of the Long Winter return
Like the breaking of brittle bones
And nightmares a frosty night

I walk through a forest
With branches covered in ice
Seeing the world at every angle
I reach a clearing somewhere
A house like a mirage
Appears before my wide open eyes
A dark lodge in the bright sunshine
The pale yellow wall turns white
And shadows fill the air

I walk through hallways filled with mist
The chill in the air broken
By the tall-burning fireplaces
The boy, now a man tells tales
Of the long winter
To the astute and attentive children
Gathered in his circle

SHOT IN THE HEAD
2013-03-03

He was shot in the head
He was stone cold dead
A great fucking rhyme
From today's headlines

Like poetry in motion
The headlines invade our mind
Burrowing into our brain
Like a dull drill on overdrive

It was an unfortunate accident
The deceased drowned in beer
He couldn't swim, the poor man
Or he was too drunk to care

A man stole his dog
He was short of dinner
He cut its throat
And drank its blood

Ink is not red today
It isn't even black
But only a pervasive
Nothingness of gray

INTRICATE SPACE
2013-03-13

Dream a dream about
Traveling through intricate space
With Gila setting her traps
Strike one, strike two
Moving further on their quest

Sky above me
Earth below me
Fire within me
Mind everywhere
In my body
Ice a taste
In my gut

Gila, Boyd and the guys
Are falling down
Intricate space
Rising on its waves
To the mountain below

Intricate space is mirrors
Within mirrors moving
At every single angle
Of our burning minds
An unset world
Beyond everything
We used to know

We know the world, now
Beyond niceties and specs
The traps spring
And we feast on our game
We are hunters
We hunt ourselves

We stand on the shore
Beneath Nix Olympia
On the mountaintop below
And existence is ours
To play with
As we wish.

The darkest gleam
2013-05-05

I once met a lost girl
And squeezed her dry
I taught her about life
And made her feel joy

The little girl lost came to me
At a bright, sunny day without clouds
I spotted her as she turned a corner
She smiled to me with the darkest gleam
Of her deep-saturated eyes

I once found a lost girl
And drenched her cold
I taught her freedom
And bliss beyond words

No rules
2013-05-10

We ride the rollercoaster at night
At the edge of the road to nowhere
There are two paths ahead of us
Devil-may-care we choose the third
Or the sixth or eight or fifteenth
Six-hundred-and-ninety-fifth

They say there are rules governing our lives
That we are regulated, stamped and boxed
Screw that, we choir, as we ride the wave
To the faraway, foreign beach
Where no one has ever gone before us

We hunt the wilderness of joy and fire
We chase our prey through the blackest night
Nature has no boundaries, and neither have we
With three choices of doom, we choose neither
On a beach far away, close as a breath
We live the life we are born to live

Fire
2013-07-01

I'm high on my own supply of life and fire, FIRE
On trees dancing in the forest
From the wind moving my branches
From stars above, flames below
It's all there, whispering in the shadows

So little it takes, to see everything
So much there is to see, in one glance
I walk the forest trail, there's no trail
No railroad, no fixed tracks
I go where the dance leads me
And sometimes I take a turn and fly
I dive into the Earth in a glow of dark

Three clicks west of nowhere, I see everything
At the end of the world, right there at its center
Two times seven, I love the number seventy-seven
The rain is coming, heating my warm veins
Three clicks, five howls, joy abundant

Remembering what we'll never forget
2013-07-13

Silent people
Spoke to her
Like invisible figures
Appeared to her

It's all so clear, now
What always was
In a glimpse of shadow
In a glow turned to flame

Strings played on the
Silent movie of today
Scream to the woman
As the guitar player
Chops his strings to pieces
As the author
Sets his pages on fire

The woman, the girl that was
Smiles her great smile
Others cannot fathom

The Darkening
2013-03-25

A flower opens
Glowing in shadow
The vision clears
Revealing all the
Dark flowers of mankind

The dark cold moon
Floats in empty Space
A brave Wanderer
Findings its way
Wherever it walks

His words, echoing in daylight
Tell stories of the unknown
The misplaced and forgotten
She whispers in our ears
Tales of secrets and life

My day begins when
The daystar turns to blood
When the sky turns
Dark blue and black
When a billion lights
Brighten the night

Poet's secret word

When I reread this collection I rekindle my dark passions. My poems are more than anything honoring the *night* and the savage human being.

What is misplaced is once more found. Each morning we wake up in today's dead society we lose a little bit more of what we truly are. My poetry helps me and will help you recover from that.

They are openers, shining a dark in the gray light of day, moonlight and mist and shadow and fire revealing what civilization and a thoroughly oppressive society keep from you.

When we are strongly encouraged and forced to work and stay awake during the day, where oppression is at its strongest we lose something infinitely precious.

Well, this is a place where you will find the opposite and different effect, the opposite desires and stirrings. I am proud, I am, so very proud.

I write, partly to inspire people, especially those walking the shadows to empower themselves, and at least it works for me… and also for a few others I know about. That also feels good, so very good.

These thoughts crystallized in my mind (you guessed it) late one night, but also while I was groaning half asleep after the alarm clock had sounded the next morning.

I had no intentions of writing a back cover text, for instance, but planned on only displaying the words, the subtitle «descriptions of what cannot be described».

When I reread these poems my ambitions on their behalf and on the behalf of the publication grow. Perhaps I didn't fully understand and appreciate what this was about until I read it through. And I hadn't, until recently.

But that night something… clicked and it keeps clicking.

With this all the poems I have written in English have been published, except those that came to life and dishonor in South America and Thailand in the latter quarter of 2003. They were inscribed in my Diary of a Traveling Man late 2003 paper notebook and that one is more than likely lost forever at some hot and moist beach.

I have made several attempts at recreating them, but it just doesn't work. Can I recreate the sound of the wave hitting the shore at exactly the moment I wrote a particular line, or the distinct and unique echoes of a door slamming in the soft wind from a shore in Pataya or a reef in Tierra Del Fuego? No way!

You will find strains, pieces of them in this collection, though, inevitably, since they never really go away.

I finished this two years ahead of schedule. It was done. The last poem had been engraved. The puzzle was complete, or as complete as it will be.

On the maxi collection containing all the other collections up to August 2003 I used small fonts and tight spacing in order to reduce the number of pages and the sales price. I wanted this one to be different, to be big and spacey, easy on the eyes and spirit (but demanding on the mind and heart).

This will probably, the way it looks right now at least be my last collection of poems. I have said all I can say and will say with my four hundred and thirty-one pieces of poetry, with this particular method of expression, and any more would be to repeat myself both in form and content and I try extremely hard to not do that. At this point I feel like I have covered every single piece of my interests and passions extensively. If I should even attempt to write another, it will have to be something completely different. Even ideas for single poems will be ignored if they don't bring something radically new to me.

If I live to be a hundred I will most certainly return to poetry, in one way or another, though. For now a prolonged break feels very right. What started in 1989 as hesitant and coincidental steps has at this point run its course. And it feels strange writing that, but not wrong.

The *problem* is, as you might guess, even as I sit here writing this, that the ideas keep flooding me like a waterfall.

I expected nothing less...

One Sherwood Forest
2013-07-18
210. night 12068, in the 13. year in the time of the Twilight Storm.

Other published and upcoming novels by **Amos Keppler** from
Midnight Fire Media:

The Defenseless

The two rivers meet and join in the city of Denver, becoming one...

The two dark brothers, growing up with their sister Linda in a mundane,
average suburb, a place well entrenched in modern United States and the
world, have since their moment of birth been at odds with the world... and
with each other.
Mike and Ted Cousin are not who they are. There is a mystery here, one
of birth and upbringing, one of fate. Violence and death, blood and fire
follow them all the days of their lives. The fire is resting somewhere
inside... waiting for the Spark.
Their parents know something, but are not telling it. The policeman
Mark Stewart and their aunt Trudy do, too. Everybody knows something,
pieces of the whole, but nobody knows the whole truth, nobody telling it.
The ancient power is returning to the world, a world massively suffering
from physical and spiritual poison, on the brink of collapse and a
collective tailspin suicide run without its like in human history.
Magick is returning from its long exile. Thus begins the story of the wild
beasts rising from their ashes.
The Spark is struck, horrible and terrifying.

First book of ten in the Janus Clan series: Ten stories of the wild man in
the modern world, forty years of wandering, before the Phoenix is rising
from its ashes.

ISBN 978-82-91693-08-8

Shadow Walk

The world is changing. They know this, in their core of cores, where everything moves and shifts. Night and fire have followed them all the days of their lives.

What they carry inside has always scared them, always intrigued them...

They have always felt different, apart from the crowd. And here, now, they get the confirmation they have always wanted, always yearned for, that they are truly different, a breed apart. The metamorphosis begins. Their minds, their bodies are changing in shocking and unpredictable ways, as what's on the inside is brought to the outside. And as they themselves are changing they are also changing the world.

Danger awaits them, Life awaits them, in the small, backward New England town. Magick and Mystery may be found beneath unturned stones.

People, young and old, are descending on the small, insignificant town of Northfield, New England.

Boys and girls, students at the school of Life, Seekers, yearning for what's different, what's hidden.

They're seeking within and without, high and low.

And here, in this dusty, remote place they're finding it, turning the stone, finding the strength within themselves to be themselves, to break out of confines, to the world beyond. And in time, after the initial, tentative steps, pushing down paths new and undreamed of.

And the present day order sees them for what they are... Agents of Change, a threat to any establishment, any imposed reality. The heatwave, the worst in living memory, is nothing compared to the boiling within the human heart. The Indian Summer heralds the twilight of mankind.

ISBN 978-82-91693-12-5

Your Own Fate

From The Book of Fate:
In the Book of Fate there is everything. Every incident, all times, everything that has been, that is, that will ever be, everything that might be, everything that could have been.

But who is writing it? Who is penning it? Who is turning page by page, too many to be counted, blowing in the wind? Does it perhaps write itself, with a pen moving across the yellow sheets? Or is it a hand moving the pen, one unseen, one stretching back into the past, back to the time before everything was created, creating itself from nothing?

Timothy Joyce is an enigma, a man without a past, appearing from nowhere, to go on a rampage in an astonished world.

Jeremy Zahn is hunting Timothy Joyce. It seems like he has always been hunting him, from old London, from the island of angels, where it is said they met for the first time, to the city of angels, California, the new world.

Here, on this shaky ground, following confrontations spanning the globe, its time and space the two will fight for the last time.

And the world is watching, its people shivering in their frozen hearts.

ISBN 978-82-91693-05-7

Night on Earth

This is said to be the age of enlightenment and reason...
A culmination of thousands of years' development and illumination.

The hunters are dying off, they say. Their day is done, in favor of the new, enlightened time of neon lights, technology and civilization.

But a hunter is stalking the streets of London. A creature without form, eyes and skin. In a city on the brink of chaos, of social and economic collapse, it is stalking cops, killing them in ever more horrible ways. Sheila Watts is a hunter. She's a cop.

Sheila is lost, losing herself further by the second. She's losing herself, finding herself, as she's closing in on the creature of the night, as it is closing in on her.

Sheila Watts can taste the sweet blood in her mouth...

ISBN 978-82-91693-07-1

Dreams Belong to the Night

New, emerging urban rebel guerilla groups, freedom fighters, called terrorists by enraged authorities are overwhelming Europe.

What is, in truth terrorism? Who does it to whom?
How much can a human being take of bondage, injustice, degradation and destruction of spirit... before being fed up?

Present day society is a wound not closing.
In a modern world society destroying everything making life worth living there are those, who, through coincidence and fate, have decided not to take it anymore.
And as they are making that decision, together and as individuals, they are also starting on a journey, a journey back to humanity's roots.
Judith, Sivert, Kim, Willhelm, Anya and many more.
A handful of people against an entire world.

This is their story...

ISBN 978-82-91693-11-8

Experience the defeat of civilization, of tyranny, of anti-life in:

Thunder Road - Book One: Ice and Fire

Damon Terrill is the Storm Child. He is born into the life hostile civilization's last years, as humanity starts on its return to nature, return to Life.

It started with the need for Freedom, the passion of life, and went from there, in new and unforeseen directions, in one, final attempt to get it right.

– It's the human being's path through life, Anya told them. – What challenges, destroys and strengthens it.

The Thunder Road is making a turn. It always is. Burning Ice, Biting Flame...that is how life began. And that's how it will renew itself. No matter where humans are going. And now the blade is laid bare, ready to be tempered once more. Humanity's idiocy, their hubris has finally and fully been visited upon them. The End Time, the final hour, Ragnarok is here. The sea is rising, winds are increasing in strength. A thoroughly rotten society is collapsing under its own weight.

Humans are natural nomads. Now they become nomads anew, pulled together in small tribes once more, pulled into a fellowship of fate in a final, desperate attempt to survive, to live the life humans are born to live. Finally. Damon, Anya, Andrè, Myriam and many others have started on their way Home.

To be published June 21, 2015

AFTERGLOW DUST

She has died a million times…

Someone is stalking her. She knows this, knows it at the edge of her vision, where nothing really is seen, only dreamed. Her nightmares give her no peace. She turns and looks behind her. There is nothing there her eyes can see. But in the wind she can hear the wailing cry, the cry of Death. Sniffing that wind, she can smell the blood in her nostrils.

There is truth in flesh, they say… and there is truth in that. But there is also substance in what cannot be seen, cannot be touched. Claws and fangs cut ceaselessly through the night, looking for her. A silent cry is heard in the dark.

Someone… or something is stalking her.

She remembers a kind touch and a slap in the face, and hardly anything else.

Kathryn Caldwell is Afterglow, a woman of undetermined age, a strange creature wandering the dark corners of the world. Something happened to her once, something horrible, something she can never forget or put out of her mind. It is haunting her every second of her dark days, every moment of her pitiful sleep. She has become an empty shell, a pale imitation of the human being she once was. Long ago, as she measures time, she lost everything valuable in a human being, saw it fall through a crack, irreversible, never to be found again.

So she is wandering the darkened streets of the modern world, aimlessly, adrift, hardly ever seen, hardly ever there. People cannot see her, but she is there, present in their daily lives, an open wound that will never close.

No one is safe for Afterglow…

To be published April 30, 2014

FALLING

She can not rid herself of it, the sense of falling. It is lurking in her dreams, every time she looks at the world from the edge of her vision. The old, cruel oracle at the fair did not tell her anything she did not know.

Janet of the Blue Flame is born a sorcerer, one with powers of the mind and the body far exceeding those of most others, one in a line reaching far back in antiquity.

In this modern age she, like many others is virtually unaware of the potential resting in the murky parts of her being. She may know, deep down, but she is not aware… not until the day Malone the Sorcerer comes for her.

Malone is dark and powerful. His skills and might are unquestionable. His power speaks to her, to her murky depths, roaring in her consciousness like a storm. Janet is only Sweet Sixteen and is overwhelmed in Malone's presence. When he offers to train her, for her to become his apprentice she consents with an eagerness of a mule chasing the carrot. He is everything she is not, everything she has ever dreamed of being. She leaves her friends and family, leaves behind everything she knows and joins the mighty and enigmatic sorcerer on his quest. His harsh teaching takes her far away, into the nine realms and beyond.

He gives her her devours, gives her everything he promised and more, wishing her good luck, leaving her to pick up the pieces of her life.

Janet of the Blue Flame is ready for the world.

To be published October 31, 2015

www.ingramcontent.com/pod-product-compliance
Lightning Source LLC
Chambersburg PA
CBHW060422100426
42812CB00030B/3278/J